THE AbSmart
FITNESS PLAN

THE AbSmart
FITNESS PLAN

The Proven Workout to Lose Inches and Strengthen Your Core Without Straining Your Back

ADAM WEISS, D.C.

New York   Chicago   San Francisco   Lisbon   London   Madrid   Mexico City
Milan   New Delhi   San Juan   Seoul   Singapore   Sydney   Toronto

Library of Congress Cataloging-in-Publication Data

Weiss, Adam, D. C.
    The absmart fitness plan : the proven workout to lose inches and strengthen your core without straining your back / Adam Weiss.
       p.   cm.
    Includes bibliographical references and index.
    ISBN 13: 978-0-07-159805-7 (alk. paper)
    ISBN 10: 0-07-159805-7 (alk. paper)
    1. Reducing exercises.   2. Abdominal exercises.   3. Weight loss.   I. Title.

RA781.6.W45   2009
613.7′12—dc22
                                                              2008034457

1 2 3 4 5 6 7 8 9 10 11 12 13 14 15 16 17 18 19 20 21 22 23 24 DOC/DOC 0 9 8

ISBN 978-0-07-159805-7
MHID   0-07-159805-7

Interior photos by Wesley Park

McGraw-Hill books are available at special quantity discounts to use as premiums and sales promotions or for use in corporate training programs. To contact a representative, please visit the Contact Us pages at www.mhprofessional.com.

This book is for educational purposes. It is not intended as a substitute for individual fitness, health, and medical advice. Please consult a qualified health care professional for individual health and medical advice. The information given is designed to help you make informed decisions about your body and health. The suggestions for specific foods, nutritional supplements, and exercises in this program are not intended to replace appropriate or necessary medical care. Before starting any exercise program, always see your physician. If you have specific medical symptoms, consult your physician immediately. If any recommendations given in this program contradict your physician's advice, be sure to consult your doctor before proceeding. Mention of specific products, companies, organizations, or authorities in this book does not imply endorsement by the author or the publisher, nor does mention of specific companies, organizations, or authorities in this book imply that they endorse the book. The author and the publisher disclaim any liability or loss, personal or otherwise, resulting from the procedures in this program. Neither the author nor McGraw-Hill shall have any responsibility for any adverse effects arising directly or indirectly as a result of information provided in this book. Internet addresses and references given in this book were accurate at the time the book went to press.

    Product pictures, trademarks, and trademark brand names are used throughout this book to inform the reader about various proprietary products and trademarks and are not intended to benefit the owner of the products and trademarks and are not intended to infringe upon trademark, copyright, or other rights nor imply any claim to the mark other than that made by the owner. No endorsement of the information contained in this book has been given by the owners of such products and trademarks, and no such endorsement is implied by the inclusion of product pictures or trademarks in this book.

This book is printed on acid-free paper.

Dedicated to my family:
Dad, Mom, my wife, and my kids

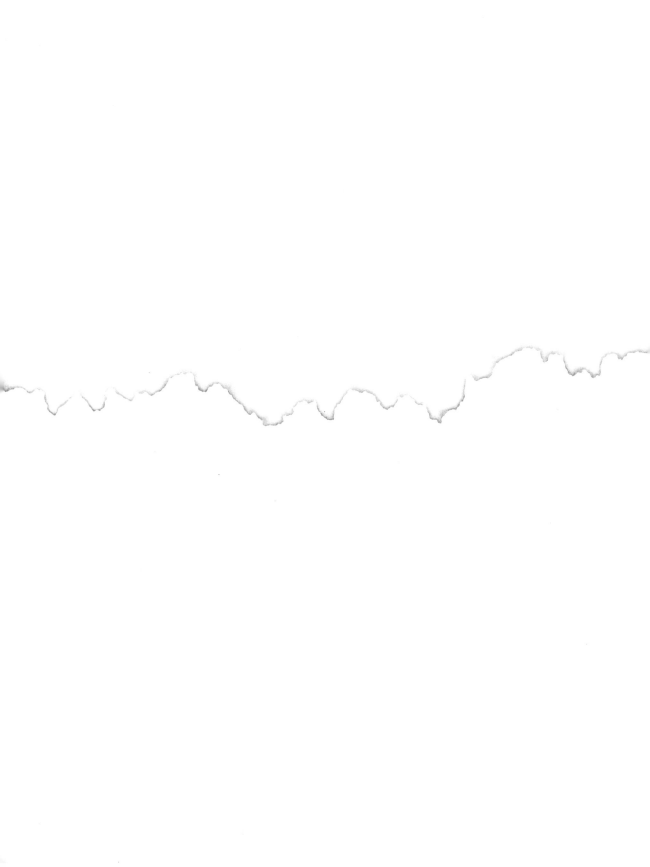

CONTENTS

ACKNOWLEDGMENTS

This book never would have seen the light of day if it weren't for the support and commitment of others. They include, first and foremost, my family. I am grateful to my mother, a true inspiration to people of all ages and someone who gives her grandchildren a run for their money while hiking up Pinnacle Peak in Scottsdale, Arizona. Keep on going, Mom!

Thanks also to my father, who constantly entertains me with his quick wit and sense of humor. He can make me smile and laugh in any situation.

Much gratitude goes to my wife. She is always there for me and keeps a sense of humor no matter what challenges we face in life.

My two children are what keep me going. I offer them a special thank you for waiting patiently for me to complete my writing. In addition, I appreciate my son, Brandon, for sharing childhood experiences with me each and every time he steps onto the mat in the dojo while I write a chapter for this book. Rachel, my daughter, I appreciate for trying new things, for laughing when she sees that her father can still do a tripod position, and of course for reminding me that I don't have to read the labels on everything I eat while on vacation.

Besides my family, I am grateful to my agent, Andrew Zack, for his determination, guidance, and support for this project; my editor, Sarah Pelz, for her support and foresight; all of the McGraw-Hill team that made this project what it is today; the models, Jackie and Kristy; and Wesley, my photographer, for helping me demonstrate the movements with ease.

In addition, I owe a debt of gratitude to my patients, who trusted me and my methods of care with each challenge they brought my way. I also thank the Pilates gang for allowing me to experiment by trying out my new exercises with them in class. This group rose to the challenge each and every time. Finally, thanks to you, my readers, for inspiring me to continue writing on the subject of exercise and for sending your supportive e-mails.

INTRODUCTION

How often have you admired the midsection of a model on a magazine cover or on TV? No question, a well-defined set of abs is appealing. But just wanting a six-pack isn't enough. You've got to put together the right combination of exercises, determine the number of sets and repetition ranges to perform, and train the muscles frequently enough to elicit results—and just about everyone has a different opinion about what works best! Moreover, it's not as if you can just do the exercises and be done; you have to watch what you put into your mouth and burn enough calories to see your results.

Women and men have been trying to lose weight and get their waistlines flatter, smaller, and stronger for years. Their reasons vary: some want to look and feel better to become more appealing and attractive, others take up exercising their midsection because they hope to prevent back pain, and some people do it as conditioning for sporting events. What the majority of these folks have in common is that they stop before achieving their ultimate goal of losing weight and firming up their stomach region. If you're one of the people who have given up in the past, your frustrations are shared with millions of others who are trying to shed unwanted pounds and remove the spare tire from around their belt line.

ANALYSIS OF A TYPICAL PERSON'S BODY-SCULPTING ATTEMPT

If you're like most people, you are burned out from a hectic lifestyle. Therefore, your fitness plan is to obtain the maximum amount of information in the shortest period of time from magazines, TV sound bites, whatever worked best for your neighbor, or that late-night infomercial claiming you can have a skinny supermodel waistline in only minutes a day if you simply use their information.

In today's time-sensitive society, in which we are reluctant to commit personal time to ourselves, the overstressed majority of people endeavor to cram it all in at once in little packages of effort, with unsatisfactory results. Many have tried Atkins and other high-protein diets, as well as some of the trendy Mediterranean lifestyle diets—all geared toward quick, substantial weight loss. But many who have tried these diets for months found that their midsections were no firmer than when they first started; as a matter of fact, they lost a lot of muscle tissue and size in their legs, arms, and chest regions long before their midsections began to get smaller.

Why This Attempt Did Not Work

The reason for this result is that the abdominal (visceral) region, along with the hips and buttocks, stores the body's fat for the longest time, and the lesser fatty regions actually become smaller due to muscle atrophy!

These dieters may have even taken the next step and begun endless daily crunches, proud of the number of repetitions they could complete. But all the while, they were straining and tightening the wrong muscles around their core region, resulting in further injuries and dissatisfaction with their waist sizes.

Why were they, like millions of others, not achieving their goals of smaller waistlines? They may have been dieting, doing aerobics, lifting weights, working their midsections, and even endangering their lives by taking dreaded diet enhancement pills (uppers, basically, to stimulate their already overstressed adrenal glands and hormone systems to no avail). However, they probably left out major components of effective strengthening and reduction of their midsections. I propose to teach you those components. This book will explain how to achieve a flatter, stronger midsection without injuring yourself or starving in the process of reaching your goals—whether those goals include a smaller waistline, more energy, or simply a healthier lifestyle full of activities to share with your friends and loved ones.

The steps laid out in this book are truly functional methods, well-supported by clinical trials from a pooling of thousands of people of both genders and different shapes, sizes, and ages who did the AbSmart exercises and followed the recommended dietary plan to achieve a better, stronger, slimmer core. The people in these trials are real people, just like you, who don't have a lot of time in their busy schedule to waste. They wanted to lose weight in the most efficient and simplest manner possible, and the information in this book showed them how to do it right.

HOW THE ABSMART SYSTEM IS DIFFERENT

What makes this approach different from the rest of the popular exercise systems today? *The AbSmart Fitness Plan* addresses the age-old problems of the waistline by focusing on the overly constricted hip flexor muscle groups, which inhibit the proper and effective range of motion in the abdominal region. To truly exercise your midsection, these muscle groups need to be more flexible; otherwise, even if you crunch your abdominal transverse rectus muscles until the cows come home, you will be no further ahead than when you started. This book will teach you the mechanisms and sequences of how to exercise your midsection without stagnating or damaging your muscles.

Avoid the Bloat

Another way that this book is different is that the AbSmart system addresses a common and problematic issue: bloating, which results in a larger than normal waistline, regardless of the exercises performed. This is not only a female dilemma; bloating occurs at an alarming rate among men, women, and children equally on a daily basis. The causes result from our modern lifestyle, daily food consumption, and a lack of the proper and vital microorganisms that live inside our gastrointestinal tract being attacked hourly by the foods, chemicals, additives, sodium, and sugars we consume.

Without addressing the causes of bloating and the need for good microorganisms, none of the diet regimens such as low-glycemic, carbohydrate, or high-protein foods will shrink your waistline. I will show you how to prevent and reverse this damaging effect on your body with simple dietary adjustments anyone can follow.

Go Beyond the Crunch

Third, other exercises for tightening and firming the midsection are far more effective and more challenging than the standard crunch movement. I have been teaching conditioning seminars nationwide for more than 15 years, helping thousands of people achieve their weight loss goals while stimulating their workout programs, especially for their midsections, with key exercises. I will share these exercises in this book so that you, too, can reduce your waistline and tone, shape, and strengthen your core region while improving your overall health along the way.

By following the AbSmart dietary guidelines, you can lose from 10 to 15 pounds in a 10-week period by following easy, habit-forming steps to stick with and achieve your goals. I am dedicated to helping time-challenged people lose weight and keep it off while improving their lifestyle and avoiding injuries. In this book, I will reveal what I have shown thousands of my patients and fitness clients to help them intelligently lose weight and tighten their waistline with nontraditional methods of exercise using stretching, body-weight-only movements, and functional exercises that will stimulate workouts while providing a fun and challenging program regardless of starting fitness level.

THE ABSMART SYSTEM

This program is right for any frustrated person who has been trying to lose that spare tire, while also challenging the more seasoned athlete who is looking for a more effective means of slimming down and getting fitter and healthier. The AbSmart system is also designed for those of us who suffer from the fast-food, fast-paced lifestyle and are looking for something unique and effective that fits into their busy schedule. This book will offer guidance and performance improvement for the athletic reader trying to maintain a competitive edge, while simultaneously aiding the middle-aged executive trying to win the battle of the bulge.

This book offers a solid foundation of shared knowledge and proven techniques for training your abdominals. No gimmicks, no gadgets, no miracles—just proven results. You'll progress from a modest group of exercises to a more robust workout combining different angles and resistance movements to sculpt and tone your midsection. You'll see and feel results as you progress from one exercise to the next. Whether you are a longtime exerciser or just starting a regular abdominal routine after a long absence or an injury, this routine will fit your needs and give you optimal results.

THE AbSmart
FITNESS PLAN

PART I

Getting Started

CHAPTER 1

WHY ABSMART FITNESS WORKS

This book is designed to eliminate much of the guesswork about training your midsection. You can do any of the exercises as described or in countless variations—and you can perform them at home or in the gym, because no special resistance equipment is required. But as with any challenging endeavor, you've got to want it bad enough. Starting wherever you are today, simply build upon each workout to achieve your goal. Continue to strive for excellence, and you'll be astonished at the progress you have the power to make.

These exercises can be challenging. It will take time for you to perform them correctly and smoothly. Be patient; there is a learning curve, and each person performs and starts at a different physical level. After each training session, you will have discovered that you are getting stronger and more flexible, so you can perform the exercises with greater ease. Don't become discouraged if you are unable to raise your legs as high or bring your upper body up as far as the person demonstrating the exercise in the photographs. Remember, your range of motion and your strength directly affect your ability to have complete control of your body's movement when performing the exercise.

I hope you will allow me to coax you into realizing your personal potential to surpass your previous goals for your midsection routine. Besides maintaining a full-time practice seeing patients, I teach more than 25 hours a week of conditioning classes and Pilates reformer classes, fine-tuning exercises that allow one to work very precisely to develop core strength, flexibility, and good alignment while exercising, applying the exercises in this book every day. The people in my classes range from those who are very fit to those who have not exercised in more than a decade. All have benefited from the AbSmart system by staying focused and doing the movements with clean, controlled effort. You, too, will see and feel results in a short time if you stay consistent.

This is not a spot reduction book; rather, it will teach you the most effective way to train smarter to achieve a stronger midsection and core. Your abdominal muscles serve a purpose far greater than that of making you look good. This section of our body is vital to our well-being, because the core is the body's last region to give up our fat storage protecting our vital organs. Together with the muscles of your lower back, your midsection forms a natural barrier around your whole waistline. When contracted, these muscles increase your intra-abdominal pressure, protecting and enhancing the stability of your spinal region. Strong abdominals promote good posture and a stronger, healthier body as a whole.

WHY I CREATED ABSMART

I wrote this book for three major reasons. First, it's an alternative for those who are tired of doing the same exercises for the abdominal muscles while lying on the floor and for those who think they have to do endless amounts of repetitions upon repetitions of the same exercises, set after set to get a firmer waistline. You'll be happy and surprised to know that you don't have to! This book offers a more efficient approach.

The second reason is to show individuals who have suffered from injuries how they can improve core strength to help stabilize this important region. These are the people I see daily in my office after they have sustained some type of injury. This reason is also close to my heart because pain and exercise brought me to study chiropractic medicine in the first place. For more than half of my life, I have been in some form of pain that reduced my training ability or completely stopped me from exercising altogether for months at a time. While it would be nice to say I have found all the answers to my aches and pains and the perfect exercises for everyone, that would be misleading. Rather, I like to think I have shown thousands of people for more than 15 years how the AbSmart system of exercising is an intelligent and functional way to exercise that allows people to personalize and use the system to enhance their body and strengthen their core, thus reducing the occurrence of injuries while improving the way they feel and look.

My experience has also taught me why the midsection more than any other body part is worth exercising. In fact, I started training my abs not for looks or injury prevention, but for martial arts competition. During my teens, I needed a strong midsection to absorb the blows that occurred while sparring with my opponents. I would do hundreds and hundreds of repetitions throughout the day from the time I woke up to the time I went to sleep. I would sneak in quick sets of abdominal exercises whenever I could. Not only did strong abs protect me, but they also helped me develop a strong core for kicking and punching. But while I was in high school, I injured my back and then went for months without working my midsection. For the first time, I became weak in a region where I had always been strong. After years of struggling with this weakness, I began retraining and changing the angles to work my midsection more effectively. My friends began training with me and trying these new movements, and they too started to see and feel stronger abs as a result of these new exercises. To this day, regardless of age or fitness level, anyone who does these AbSmart exercises can feel and see results, because rather than isolating a single muscle group, the AbSmart program uses functional movements to engage multiple muscle groups in an integrated way, synergizing the entire body in a challenging total-body workout. Although genetics might play some role in how we look, genetics doesn't make up for perseverance and determination.

It would be nice to say that this is where my problems ended and simply present you with the system for a stronger waistline. However, over the years, I had many misfortunes that affected my strength and the size of my midsection. I was struck with another injury in my early thirties. I was again training and competing in the martial arts, when I was struck by daily lower-abdominal pain for months. After many tests and procedures, I was told I had a large inguinal hernia in my lower abdominal region. It needed to be repaired immediately before my intestine became pinched off and obstructed.

After surgery, I was unable to exercise my midsection for nearly half a year; I began to gain weight and again became weaker in the midsection. I had to adapt my abs exercises not only for back problems but also so I would not strain the abdominal wall, which would result in days of pain and discomfort. One year after the first surgery, I was struck by severe upper-abdominal pain. This time I was told my gallbladder was no longer functioning; stones were building up and then passing painfully through my gastrointestinal (GI) system. I went back under the knife and had to deal with incisions and scar tissue in my midsection that had to heal. Without a gallbladder, I needed to adjust my diet in order to fend off the excessive bloating and swelling that tend to accompany the bile that would now go unchecked from my liver. This is very common in people who have gallbladder disease or have had this organ removed.

As you can see, not only did I need to retrain my abdominals from the outside, I also needed to take care of myself from the inside. Based on what I learned, I include in this book the foods and diet tips that have helped me and thousands of my clients—male and female—who suffer from GI discomfort, bloating, and cramping. What became crystal clear to me through all these unfortunate events was that if I wanted stronger abs and to be healthy and fit, I could no longer just exercise. I also needed to use foods in a healing way. This is what I offer you: a more effective way to exercise and eat to a slimmer midsection.

The third reason I wrote this book is to show that you do not have to have inherited the natural gift of a strong midsection to exercise this region, nor do you need the perfect lifestyle or setting to achieve the results you want. You can do as many exercises as you want using the AbSmart system. If you do that and eat smartly, you will get results.

HOW TO USE THIS BOOK

This book is meant to be used as a total program to tone and strengthen your midsection. You'll notice that I don't specify the number of repetitions and sets to perform for each exercise. That's because I've read and tested numerous methods and studies on how many repetitions are necessary to get results, how to train different muscle fibers to stimulate fast-twitch and slow-twitch muscle fibers, and how long it should take someone to complete the movements, whether the person is a competitive athlete or has not exercised in years. The results were clear: no matter what shape you are in, repetitions and sets can be only a rough guide. For some exercises, you may need to do 15 to 20 repetitions before you feel your muscles working, while you might feel another movement right away and complete only 8 or 10 repetitions before stopping your set. I address this topic more in Chapter 8, where I help you personalize the AbSmart program and create an abs routine that works for you.

The AbSmart system is—for lack of a better word—a holistic approach to exercising and strengthening your core. As you become stronger, you achieve a better mind and muscle connection, and as you progress, you'll perform the movements with less effort or for longer before feeling fatigue.

When you use the AbSmart system of targeted abdominal exercises and clinically proven diet advice to define and shrink your midriff with honest effort, you will be proud of yourself and your results. The following chapters will show you step by step how to improve your exercises for your midsection and how to combine your food groups to get the body shape you desire.

Let's get started!

CHAPTER 2

WHY CRUNCHES DON'T GET THE JOB DONE

I've noticed that the younger generations have weaker cores than those who were growing up ten years ago did, and I am seeing younger and younger patients with sports injuries related to weaker core muscle groups. At the same time, the baby boomers are starting to work out more frequently, using heavy equipment in gyms to work their core regions and injuring themselves while using these machines for performing the crunch movement.

Over the years, most of my patients' injuries related to sports and exercise in general were the result of misalignment and a weak core. In most cases, these misalignment issues had developed over years of improper form or overexertion in one particular plane of motion. In this chapter, I will point out the most common errors, so you can avoid making similar mistakes or can change bad habits you may have developed already. In that way, you can improve your abdominal strength and shape while preventing injuries.

The AbSmart approach to abdominal improvement is a progressive way of training. Rather than simply telling someone how to do an exercise, the AbSmart system approaches each person and personalizes the exercise to her or his shape, size, and goals. For example, when you observe two people performing the same movement, you might see that one person can do it more easily while the other one struggles. Does this mean the latter is weaker? Not necessarily. What works for one type of person doesn't necessarily work for a similarly built person, even if they have the same age, weight, and fitness level. Therefore, you will learn to analyze commonly overlooked restrictions and limitations to performing this abdominal exercise and how your body mechanics may be hindering the way you are performing the movements. I'll show how to improve upon the exercise so you can perform the movement more effectively, regardless of shape or gender.

The AbSmart system is in a constant state of change. Once you learn the movements, you will be varying your workout routine to strengthen your core. This chapter explores different techniques and discusses how to avoid injuries and pitfalls that could set you back from your progress.

This chapter will challenge the way you think about your body and the way you move through your abdominal workouts. It will also encourage you to exercise in a healthier and more functional way to enhance your workouts and outcome.

THE PROBLEM WITH CRUNCHES: MISALIGNMENTS

A misalignment occurs when a body part (particularly the hip flexors, back, shoulders, or neck) is held or used in a way that it was not designed or intended for and is forced through an unnatural range of motion. This should not be mistaken for the feeling of discomfort you get when stretching a tight muscle group or the way you feel after working out after a long layoff, when your muscles are sore from the lack of use rather than straining. How many times have you felt a strain in your neck or in your lower or middle back while performing the crunch or any other abdominal exercise? Did it happen because your abs were too weak to perform the action, or were you compensating for tight muscle groups? Perhaps the exercise was wrong for your body type, or you might have been trying to force yourself through an unnatural range of motion, causing an imbalance between your abdominal muscles and your opposing and secondary muscles.

As you can see, there are many reasons why a certain exercise doesn't feel right while you are performing the movement. What was intended to be an isolating exercise for your abdominal region is no longer so because your inflexible muscles are hindering your ability to feel the right muscle groups for that particular movement for your abdominal muscles.

With these drawbacks, how did the crunch become the go-to exercise for the abdominal region in the first place? I have a strong feeling that before universities and professional sports teams began using this movement, it evolved in the mid-1980s, when people began participating in step aerobics classes and removing the incline sit-up boards in the gyms. You see, when people were doing step or dance movements, they were getting their heart rates up, and then they would lie down on the floor to work their abs as part of a cool-down routine or as a warm-up, depending on the instructor, without using any special equipment. They also were not going to start holding each other's ankles while the other person performed the sit-up movement.

Only a few could perform a full sit-up without assistance, while the majority would, instead, lift their feet off the floor as they threw themselves upward toward their bent knees with their upper-body strength and then dropped down from the effort. This throwing upward and dropping down caused misalignments of the neck and lower-back regions. Not surprisingly, many people performing sit-ups developed lower-back problems and strained this vulnerable region. To reduce the number of casualties in the exercise classes, instructors began teaching exercisers to keep the lower back flat and raise their upper body only high enough to feel the abdominal muscles contract, then lower it to the beginning position.

The instructors were also conscious of the weakened neck region because people began to complain of neck strains when performing this crunch. Thus, they adopted the expression "Think of an apple or orange between your chest and under your chin," so exercisers would keep their neck from flexing forward. In the medical world, we call this an "anterior" head carriage position, which causes stress to the nerve roots coming off the spine on the sides of the neck region.

This change further limited the resistance on the abdominal region, because most people kept their elbows too far back while performing the crunch, making sure not to push the head forward past that invisible apple barrier that may cause the person to pull too far forward, resulting in straining the neck. Unfortunately, that also meant they did not challenge their abs as much as they could, making it a less effective exercise. For some people to make this movement more effective, their elbows should be in front of their head while supporting the neck, keeping the natural curve of the spine in place; for others, their arms are just to rest their head on.

You need to experiment with not only your abdominal exercises but also your hand positions within the movement itself to provide you with the maximum benefit and feel of your muscles exercising smoothly. Later on in the book, I give details on choosing the best arm position to enhance your conditioning when performing abdominal exercises.

BUT IT FEELS LIKE IT'S WORKING

You might wonder why you feel your abs cramping up and fatiguing after a set of crunches. Doesn't this mean you're working your abs to the maximum and effectively? Think of a balloon being blown up by a child versus an adult. A child trying to blow air into a balloon exerts more effort and needs more time to enlarge the balloon, while an adult, with a larger lung capacity, can blow longer and stronger into the balloon, expanding it much more quickly. Similarly, the limited range of motion in the crunch exercise as it is performed by most people stretches the smooth and contractual muscle fibers in the abdominal region, simultaneously pooling the blood rapidly in the region. Similar to the balloon, once the muscle has reached its maximum size, it can no longer expand the abdominal muscles. As a result, the person experiences fatigue, and any further attempts at repetitions become dysfunctional at best. This is why you cannot gauge your progress based on how you feel during a particular exercise.

Along those lines, if you simply raise your head a few inches off the ground until just the top of your shoulders come off the ground and then return to the starting position, you are not giving yourself the opportunity to work the deep tissues along the full length of your abdominal region. Would you only curl halfway up for your biceps during a bicep curl or do only half a range of motion on your bench press? See my point? If you only train in a short range of motion, you are developing less of the body part and setting yourself up for possible injury when using that region of your body.

THE IMPORTANCE OF LEG POSITION

One of the key elements of maintaining proper spinal alignment and minimum hip flexor involvement at the beginning of your workouts is placement

THE TROUBLE WITH CRUNCHES: LEANNE'S STORY

Leanne was a 44-year-old karate enthusiast who had trained for more than 20 years, experiencing multiple injuries along the way. Over the past three years, her neck had started to give her problems to the extent that she would have to take off weeks at a time. She was eventually diagnosed with a disc injury, so she was forced to adapt her martial arts techniques. Although this change helped her, she continued to get bouts of neck pain. After discussing her cross-training outside of her martial arts, I learned she performed abdominal exercises every day before training to keep her midsection strong. I asked her to show me her abdominal routine. She proceeded to lie on the floor with her knees bent, feet on the floor, and hands behind her head.

As she inched her way up for countless repetitions, I noticed a number of key issues and began pointing them out to her. First, she kept her legs apart when performing the classic crunch and her knees bent too much, overstimulating her hip flexors much more than her abdominal region. Second, I noticed she was not coming far enough forward to activate her entire abdominal region. Third, she was forcing her head forward in that anterior head position, so she was straining her neck muscles while performing the classic crunch.

As an athlete and, more importantly, a martial artist, she understood the importance of being flexible in all her muscle groups for the best results. I showed her a number of stretches for her hip flexors and ways to perform other abdominal exercises first to strengthen and tone her lower abdominal region. "I was really surprised at how much I felt my abs after trying the stretches first, then the abdominal routine," she said. "And there was no more neck pain involved with the movements." Leanne continues to work her midsection every day, but without the pain.

of your feet. Most exercisers rest their feet on the floor with their knees bent. By doing crunches in this manner, the exerciser has eliminated more than half of the resistance to begin with. Having the lower legs below your knee level with the feet on the floor makes the workout less effective. I agree with those who say it makes the exercise easier—but why bother doing the movement and contracting your iliopsoas muscles (hip flexors) harder than the abdominal region if your goal is a firmer, smaller midsection?

Furthermore, having your feet on the ground accentuates the spinal curve, destabilizing the pelvic muscles and increasing the risk of lower-back injury, contrary to popular belief. Why is this? Your back is flat on the floor, right? But even though you are lying flat on your back, a closer look at the body mechanics and the muscle structure in the pelvic floor region shows that the tight hip flexors (iliopsoas muscles) are being placed in a contracted position, thus firing the muscle fibers and signaling a contraction long before your abdominal muscles begin the movement. Also, as

THE TROUBLE WITH CRUNCHES: SCOTT'S STORY

Scott was a 34-year-old avid runner and downhill snowboarder who just loved a challenge. He would take everything to the maximum, including his workouts in the gym. He found himself in my office complaining of lower-abdominal and back pain for the past month. After ruling out a hernia and other disease ailments, I began to ask him about his workouts. He said he did a full-body circuit with free weights and machines to keep himself strong. He also stretched before and after his runs. When he described more specifically his core workout, we began to find the cause of his lower-abdominal pain. He started his workouts on the Swiss ball and then proceeded to straight-leg raises while holding onto a chin-up bar. Next, he placed a 45-pound plate on his feet as he performed crunches until he fatigued his abs, typically after around 70 or 80 repetitions.

While impressed with his strength, I knew he was activating his hip flexors way too much and was straining his lower back in the process. We included the AbSmart stretches for his hip flexors, which he did before and after his runs in addition to abdominal exercises. In his core routine, we changed the order and moved the weights off his feet because he didn't need to have more resistance added to his own body weight to isolate his midsection. "I noticed a change in my running stride and less discomfort in my longer-distance runs at first. By the end of two months, I could really feel my abs more during my workouts and less discomfort than before," Scott said. We continue to train together, tweaking his routine as he progresses into the snowboard season.

described earlier, having the weight of your feet below your knees in this classic crunch position reduces the overall effect on the abdominal region.

ARE YOUR HIP FLEXORS TOO TIGHT?

Ask yourself these questions:

- Do you sit in a car or train to commute to work during the weekday?
- Do you sit at your job? Getting up and down all day doesn't count as being active at work; the end result is you are still flexing those muscles each time you get up out of your chair.
- Do you sit while eating your lunch?
- Do you sit commuting home from work?
- Do you sit while eating dinner?
- Do you sit while doing load-bearing exercises, such as lat pull-downs, shoulder presses, dumbbell curls, and leg extensions?

If you answered yes to a few of these questions, you might be an average person, sitting more than 10 hours a day (maybe more on the weekends), depending on your activity level. All of these factors cause your hip flexors to tighten throughout the day. As you will see in the next chapter, this key muscle group can really make or break your success in tightening and reducing your waistline.

Even if you have an active job and are on your feet all day, you are not in the clear just yet. Your hip flexors pull your pelvic muscles forward when you stand too long as well. Some people keep their feet up and rest them on a bench or ball while performing crunches, thinking they are safe to assume they are not contracting their hip flexors. While this is partially true, this practice makes your abs weaker because you are not using the weighted resistance of your lower legs. If you do more functional movements while working your midsection, you will notice a dramatic difference in your strength and the shape of your waistline.

As you can see, while the crunch exercise stimulates the midsection to the point where you feel you are unable to perform any more repetitions, in reality you are fatiguing your hip flexors first, long before your abs get tired. Although the AbSmart method has crunches for the abdominal region, you will see in the following chapters how to incorporate the crunch movement

AS SEEN ON TV

Years of packing on the weight in an area noticeable to others makes us easy marks for the late-night infomercial experts. You have probably seen an infomercial showing a thin, firm male or female model lying out by the pool and the machine somewhere indoors that supposedly did it all for him or her. Ever wonder how many of these gadgets and machines were field-tested or scientifically proven to be worth our dollars, let alone our efforts? How do these machines compare with the traditional abdominal crunch?

Researchers at Occidental College in Los Angeles put these abs devices to the test. The researchers measured the amount of stress the six leading devices seen on TV placed on the abdominal region and then compared them with the traditional abdominal crunch. The results may surprise you.

The only product to elicit a greater muscle stimulus (26 times harder) than the crunch was one that utilized a resistance band to add resistance to the traditional crunch motion. You could get the same results by doing a traditional crunch using resistance such as a dumbbell or medicine ball while performing the movement, without the additional cost. We will discuss in Chapter 7 the use of adding resistance in your exercise routine, along with guidance in who would benefit from such weighted resistance and who should avoid it at all costs.

While these various abs devices continue to sell the promise of a tighter, firmer waistline, this study proves that these machines are not necessarily the most effective use of your time for training your midsection. If you are sitting or lying down and a machine makes it easier to raise and lower your arms or legs, where is the resistance taking place? Do you really want to spend only minutes a day on such a vital and important region of your body? You want to focus on your core region as much as or even more than you would on your arms, chest, or legs. Most people don't, so they turn to gadgets that they think will speed up their results with less effort and half the time. Don't fall prey to this; instead, focus on your midsection as an investment opportunity that will pay back dividends for years to come.

The more you focus on and train this region of your body and make it a priority muscle group, the longer you will be able to maintain a healthier and stronger lifestyle, enjoying sport activities and hobbies without injuries to a well-protected, stronger core and a stronger lower back. Using a machine might be easier, and it might reduce your workout time, but will it give you the results you are really after? In the following chapters, I will show you how to exercise your midsection smarter for better results.

between exercises while training your waistline more effectively. Chapter 3 discusses improving your midsection by addressing the stretching of those tight hip flexors.

YOUR MIDSECTION ANATOMY

By understanding how each abdominal muscle functions, you'll be able to exercise your waistline more efficiently. The muscle groups in your midsection are composed of four major and interacting muscles:

- **Rectus abdominis:** Located between your sternum and your pelvis, it is responsible for your trunk flexion.
- **Transverse abdominis:** Located deep below your abdominal wall, with the fibers running horizontally or across your midsection, it primarily maintains constant firmness in this region.
- **External and internal obliques:** Located along the sides of your waistline, these muscles are used for rotation and bending to the side.
- **Intercostals:** Lying between the ribs and angling downward in the sides of the rib cage and the upper abdominal wall, these muscles come into play by flexing your torso and turning your trunk. The intercostals also help you breathe.

CHAPTER SUMMARY

- The crunch movement alone will not define and tone your midsection.
- That burning or pumped-up feeling after doing repetition after repetition is not a true sign of progress.
- Your hip flexors are inflexible; for most of us, that inhibits complete range of motion to work the abdominal region.
- Resting your feet on something while performing the movement will reduce the benefit of strengthening your waistline.

CHAPTER 3

PREPARING TO WORK OUT

Before you get started with the AbSmart workout, there are some things you need to know. This chapter will tell you how to maximize the abs-trimming effects of the workout and to prevent injury while toning your midsection.

KEYS TO A SUCCESSFUL WORKOUT

Do not let your ego overpower your technique when exercising; it takes very little effort once momentum comes into play when working your core, and you will be using other muscle groups rather than the important core muscles. Even if you do fewer reps, by not letting momentum take over you will get much better results. Focus instead on breathing and pulling in your abdominal muscles as you execute each and every exercise. This will assure you that you are getting the most out of your workouts.

Breath Control

When I'm giving seminars or teaching one of my Pilates reformer classes, many of the questions I hear are related to breath control. While you are exercising, the right way of breathing will help you stay focused, and you will be able to perform the movements for longer periods of time. Proper breathing will take time to learn, but with continued practice it will become easier, and your breathing will become more natural. You'll be in the zone, so don't worry if you are breathing at the right time when you are first learning the new exercises; as you become more comfortable with the routine, proper breathing will follow. Here are a few pointers to keep in mind:

- To breathe properly, you need to eliminate tension in your muscles while breathing.
- Breathe naturally without overemphasizing either the inhaling or exhaling component during your workouts.
- Allow your lungs to fill completely each time you inhale.
- Set a natural rhythmic breathing pattern while resting between sets.

Focus on the Movement

It seems many people avoid stomach exercises because performing them is too painful. Perhaps when these people did stomach exercises in the past, they were working against themselves rather than focusing on the flow of the movement. Instead of rushing through repetitions, you should focus on feeling the individual muscle groups, concentrating on and relaxing them when needed. Go through a full range of motion, and do not force yourself to follow any instructions in this book (or any others, for that matter) that do not suit your body specifically. Not every exercise is for everyone; if you encounter pain, stop, omit the exercise, and go on to a different one. If pain persists, seek out a medical evaluation to rule out any underlying physical problems that may be present.

Remember, it takes focus and control of your core muscles to work as a unit. Don't treat them as individual muscles that you work out on Mondays and Wednesdays; think about them all the time when you are bench pressing or swinging a golf club or tennis racket. Your midsection will become stronger if you work intelligently and progressively every day, and you will see and feel results quickly.

STRETCHING YOUR ILIOPSOAS: MAKING ABS REACT BETTER TO EXERCISE

Stretch your what? You may be asking yourself whether you even have one of these. The muscle group called the iliopsoas, or psoas, is more commonly known as the hip flexors. This muscle group lies on both sides of the front of the hips and attaches along the lower vertebrae of the spine behind the stomach region.

Why does this function make it an important muscle group when you are training your abdominals? The primary function of the psoas major muscles is flexion of the thigh at the hip. The psoas can assist extension of the lower spine there by increasing the curve in the lower back. Thus, sit-ups cause back pain for many people with tight hip flexors. During the sit-up motion, the psoas muscle is vigorously active during the last 60 degrees.

The psoas also plays a significant role in maintaining our upright posture when we are standing. In addition, the hip flexors assist in lifting our legs out to the side, away from our body, and strongly come into play during running, sprinting, and jogging.

This group is made up of very strong muscles that inhibit your range of motion when you do any form of abdominal exercises, including the crunch or reverse crunch. If these muscles are not stretched out properly, you will not benefit completely from your abdominal workout, and most likely, the effort will be fruitless because most of the muscles working will be your psoas muscles, rather than your abdominal wall. Having tight or less flexible hip flexors can set you up for future injuries to your back muscles and spine by further tightening up a muscle group that pulls the spine forward, causing deep irritation and a weaker midsection.

Why Does This Occur?

The key movement of the psoas is to maintain alignment of the body and the spine, keeping the body upright. When you are standing and sitting, this muscle group is constantly being used, until you lie flat on your back.

The reason that the psoas muscle group is overly constricted is that the Western lifestyle of too much sitting, driving, and taking the escalator brings about deconditioned muscles and chronic muscle tightness. Not moving around enough causes the muscles to stiffen and become less sup-

---

HOW COMMON BACK INJURIES HAPPEN: TED'S STORY

Ted was a 24-year-old competitive downhill skier who trained all year round. Like many top athletes, Ted knew the importance of core training and maintaining a healthy body weight. What Ted found out the hard way was that he was overtraining his hip flexors with his sport and his training workouts.

Ted came into my office during his off-season, complaining of overall muscle fatigue and soreness in his back muscles, especially his lower back region. He said he was trying to adjust his routine to fit in more power moves and abdominal exercises to help prevent injuries from occurring and improve his overall skiing. Ted's power moves included squats, clean and presses, and dead lifts. Every other day, he also performed sets of 100 crunches and leg lifts while holding a 25-pound plate. No matter how much he stretched out, his back was constantly sore and felt weak during his abdominal routine. I had him perform some basic lunges and noticed he was unable to straighten his back leg without his foot coming off the ground. This was a sure sign of tightness in the hip flexors and lower leg muscles.

We began each session by stretching out Ted's hip flexors and adjusted his power exercises to include a more balanced routine. "I couldn't believe how tight I was," Ted later went on to say. "I thought my legs were one of my stronger body parts. But after learning how to stretch them out properly, I could move more easily and felt more flexible, so I could lift heaver weights. I also learned that by using weights with my abs exercises, I was straining my hip flexors, which aggravated my back."

After one month of the AbSmart stretching for his psoas muscles and training his abs properly, Ted felt stronger and had less back pain from his routine; he returned to his competitive season in better shape.

---

ple with each growing day. Our modern lifestyle contributes to our stiff backs and weak abdominals due to the lack of proper use of these groups. We develop chronically tight hip flexors from our poor postural habits throughout the day.

How Does a Tight Psoas Affect the Abdominal Exercises?

Many times, very fit, active patients of all ages enter my office complaining of back pain after exercising their midsections. A first sign that it is coming from this region is that the patient describes the pain as running down his or her spine, rather than horizontally. Patients also complain frequently of groin pain; these types of pain are associated with back pain being aggravated when they move from a sitting position to a standing position. All are sure signs of hip flexors involved with their back pain.

GET READY TO STRETCH

Individuals with different backgrounds and training levels have all overcome their limited range of motion of their hip flexors first by stretching this complex muscle group, thus easily engaging their abdominal muscles without hindrance, resulting in more effective training. Now it's your turn to become more flexible and stronger with a firmer waistline by following these simple guidelines.

The following series of stretching exercises, meant to precede your abdominal workout, start with an easy position and progress upward toward a more advanced movement, during which you will feel a stronger stretch in the muscle groups. Depending on your overall flexibility or lack of it, you will find some movements difficult to hold at first. Over the next few weeks, as you progress in isolating this muscle group, you will feel the muscles releasing the tightness as you gain greater range of motion. Do not get discouraged by the lack of dramatic increase in your flexibility in this muscle group. Considering how easy it is to become inflexible just by walking around in our modern society, it will take time to undo all that stress to this region of your body.

HOW COMMON BACK INJURIES HAPPEN:
LESLEY'S STORY

Lesley was a 35-year-old mother of two who competed with her local swim club and raced against women 10 to 15 years younger until she injured herself while performing a flip turn in the pool. As a result of that injury, she sustained severe lower-abdominal pain and groin pain. She experienced constant pain and discomfort no matter how long she stayed out of the pool. After taking six months off, all the while continuing to train in the gym, she finally came to my center.

Lesley's posture was hunched over, and she had an exaggerated curve in her lower back, which was notable when I looked at her from the side. She said she stayed out of the pool and performed Pilates and toning classes at her local health club but still felt weak and sore months later. What we found was that she rarely stretched out her muscles except for a few toe touches and leg splits; she commented that she had had great hip flexibility all her life, so she felt lucky she didn't need to stretch as much as the rest of us. Because of her hip joint flexibility, her hip flexor muscles were tight and overcompensating to stabilize the pelvic muscles. This caused the muscles to shorten and inhibited her range of motion, which aggravated the core muscles every time she trained them. She further tightened rather than lengthened her muscles when she was training and swimming.

Lesley had great results with the AbSmart program. She said, "After performing the AbSmart psoas stretches, I could really feel my abs working and not that pulling sensation in front of my hips and groin as before." Not long after learning the stretches for her hip flexors, Lesley returned to the pool and once again competed. "I feel I am using my body much more effectively, and my muscles are in sync, rather than before, when I felt I was pulling myself through the water. Now I glide through my new workouts."

Remember to take each move slowly and to breathe deeply and relax. Do not force yourself into any uncomfortable positions. You should feel stretching, not straining, which is key to enhancing your flexibility. Hold each position for 30 seconds to 1 minute unless stated otherwise. And you can always go back to a stretch you started with again if you like. If you do, as you warm up, you will see in your first sets of exercises that you can stretch a little more easily the second time around. When you focus your energy on improving your flexibility in this muscle group, the rest of your body will improve the quality of the rest of your abdominal workout.

Psoas Stretch While Facing Chair

1. Stand facing a chair, about 2 feet away from it. Place your feet shoulder-width apart.

2. Bend your right knee, and place your right foot on the seat of the chair.

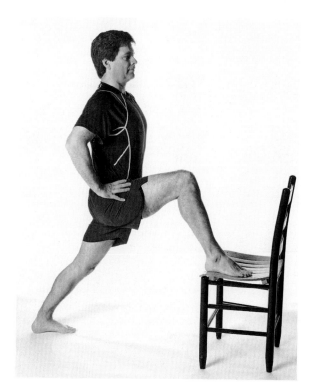

3.1
Psoas Stretch While
Facing Chair

3. Simultaneously slide your left foot back as you feel the stretch in your left leg as you move the leg backward. Keep your left leg straight during the movement. (For more of a stretch, lean forward from your waist while holding the chair with your hands for balance.)

4. Hold for 10 to 30 seconds, and slowly return to the upright position with both feet on the floor. Then repeat the movement.

5. Repeat the entire sequence on the opposite leg.

Key Points to Remember

• Place another chair next to you to hang onto or stand near a wall to help support yourself until your balance and flexibility improves.

• Balance and control are key to this movement.

• As you develop further flexibility and balance, the exercise will become easier.

Psoas Stretch with Chair Behind You

1. Stand with your back to a chair, about 3 feet away from it. Place your feet shoulder-width apart.

2. Bend your left knee, and place the top of your left foot on the chair behind you.

3. Bend slowly down toward the floor, straighten your left leg as you bend your right knee slowly down, and rest your hands on your waist.

4. Hold for 10 to 30 seconds, and slowly return to the upright position. Repeat the movement.

5. Repeat the entire sequence on the opposite leg.

3.2
Psoas Stretch with
Chair Behind You

Key Points to Remember

- Hold onto a wall or another chair for balance. As you progress, you will no longer need to support yourself.

- Balance is key to this movement.

Psoas Stretch Without Chair

1. Stand with your feet shoulder-width apart and arms resting by your waist.

2. Step forward with your right leg while bending your right knee into a lunge position, at the same time keeping your back leg straight.

3. Slowly lean your upper body forward, bending your right knee further as you increase the stretch forward. Keep your back straight. (Make sure your feet are pointing straight ahead throughout the movement.)

4. Hold for 10 to 30 seconds, and then slowly return to the upright position. Repeat the movement.

5. Repeat the entire sequence on the opposite leg.

3.3
Psoas Stretch
Without Chair

Key Points to Remember

- Hold onto a wall or a chair for balance. As you progress, you will no longer need to support yourself.

- Balance is key to this movement.

Psoas Bench Stretch

First Movement

For this movement, you will need to be high enough off the floor to feel the stretch in your hip flexors. A tall bench, table, or bed will work. Make sure you are comfortable wherever you choose to do the stretch.

1. Start by sitting at the edge of the bench. With your back straight, pull your bent right knee up toward your chest, and hold it against your chest with your hands.

2. Slowly lie back while holding your knee against your chest, and allow your left leg to hang in the air.

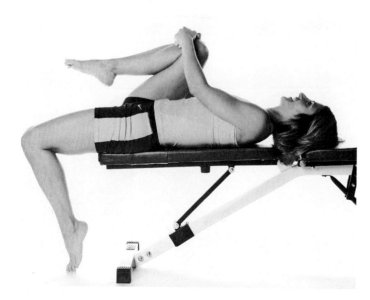

3.4
Psoas
Bench Stretch

Second Movement

1. Slowly relax your left leg down toward the floor while simultaneously pulling your right knee closer toward your chest. You should feel an increase in the stretch in your left leg when you do this.

2. Slowly move your left heel back underneath the bench. You will feel a further stretch in your left leg.

3. Hold for 10 to 30 seconds, and slowly return to the starting position. Repeat the movement.

4. Repeat the entire exercise on the opposite leg.

Wall Stretch

First Movement

1. Start on your knees about a foot away from a wall, facing away from the wall.

2. Place your hands shoulder-width apart in front of your knees.

3.5a
Wall Stretch

3. Place the top of your left foot flat against the wall with your knee bent, resting your left shin against the wall, and your left knee on the floor.

Second Movement

1. Using your arms for support and balance, move your right leg up into a lunge position. Place your hands on your right thigh to increase the stretch in your hip flexors.

2. Hold for 10 to 30 seconds, and then slowly return with your hands back on the floor.

3. Repeat the entire exercise on the opposite leg.

Key Points to Remember

• If you have a knee injury or had knee surgery, do not do this movement.

• If you feel knee pressure, check your position to make sure you have good leg alignment with your foot directly behind you and not off to the side.

3.5b
Wall Stretch

- Your front knee should be directly over your foot in the deep lunge position.

- Your body weight should not rest directly on top of your kneecap during the stretching movement. Rather, lean back into the stretch.

- If you find this position easy, bring your hands up onto the lunging knee and stretch up through your entire body.

Inner-Thigh Stretch

The reason I am including inner thigh muscles with the hip flexors is that they all tie into the groin and pelvic region, and it's very hard to differentiate between the two groups when they both contribute to overall stiffness, inhibiting range of motion.

1. Start by kneeling on the floor, resting on your elbows with your hands out to the side about shoulder-width apart. Move your knees shoulder-width apart as you support yourself on your hands.

2. Slowly bend your arms at the elbows as you rest your weight on your forearms on the floor.

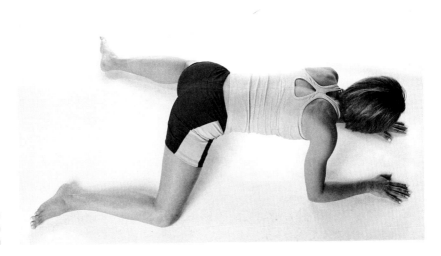

3.6
Inner-Thigh
Stretch

3. Slowly move your knees farther apart, feeling the stretch on each inner thigh.

4. Hold for 10 to 30 seconds, and slowly return to the starting position. Repeat the entire sequence.

Key Points to Remember

- If you have a knee injury or had knee surgery, do not do this movement.

- Remember not to force the movement; rather, relax into the position.

Advanced Inner-Thigh Stretch

1. Start by kneeling on the floor, resting on your forearms with your hands shoulder-width apart. Move your knees shoulder-width apart as you support yourself on your hands.

2. Slowly straighten your right leg out to the side while keeping the left knee bent.

3.7
Advanced
Inner-Thigh Stretch

3. Bend your arms at the elbows as you rest your weight on your forearms on the floor.

4. Slowly move your legs farther apart, feeling the stretch on each inner thigh.

5. Hold for 10 to 30 seconds, and slowly bend your right leg back to the starting position. Repeat the movement by moving your right leg back out again.

6. Repeat the entire sequence on the opposite leg.

Key Points to Remember

- If you have a knee injury or had knee surgery, do not do this movement.

- Make sure you are doing this movement on a firm surface, and maintain control throughout the exercise.

- Do not force the stretch; instead, relax into the position and breathe deeply.

Heel Wall Slide

1. Start by lying face up on the floor with your pelvis against the wall, your knees bent outward, and the sides of your feet against the wall, with the soles of your feet together. Your arms are resting along the sides of your body.

2. Slowly slide your feet down the wall as your knees bend out to the sides of your body. Keep your lower back flat against the floor.

3. Hold the bottom position for 30 to 60 seconds, and then return to the beginning position. Repeat the entire sequence.

Key Points to Remember

- Keep your lower back flat during the entire movement; do not raise your hips by compensating for tight lower back muscles.

- If you are unable to put the soles of your feet together, place your heels so they are touching. Over time you'll work toward putting the soles together as your feet are against the wall.

3.8a, b
Heel
Wall Slide

• To increase the stretch, use your hands to gently push down on the inside of your thighs until you feel a stretch. Relax into the position; do not force yourself into positions.

Standing Hip Stretch

This stretch will do a number of things for the advanced exerciser: stretching the hip flexors and thigh muscles while developing balance and control of your core muscles at the same time.

1. Start by standing with your feet shoulder-width apart or farther.

2. Slowly bend at your waist as you lean forward over your left foot. Place your left hand on the floor in front of your foot while simultaneously raising your right leg straight out to the side until your leg is parallel to the floor and even with your hip height.

3. Reach with your right hand, bend your right leg, and grasp your right ankle or foot while maintaining the balanced position. Bend your right arm at the elbow as you bring your right foot toward your backside while resting your weight on your left leg.

3.9
Standing Hip Stretch

4. Slowly move your right knee up farther above your waistline to increase the stretch in your right thigh and hip flexors as well as your left hamstring muscle group.

5. Hold for 10 to 30 seconds, and slowly return to the starting position. Repeat the movement on the opposite leg.

Key Points to Remember

• Keep your lower back flat during the entire movement; do not arch your back when you raise your leg to compensate for tight lower back muscles.

• If you are unable to touch the floor due to tight leg or back muscles or unable to balance yourself while holding this position, you can place your hand onto a chair in front to stabilize yourself during the exercise.

You should feel that you have stretched out your hip flexors completely at this stage. You are now ready to exercise your abdominals and core muscles properly, without any tight hip flexors inhibiting your true range of motion, so you will get better results.

Remember, if you are not feeling your abdominals properly when doing the midsection routine, check the flexibility of your psoas group first. You may have to stretch these muscles in between exercises in your core routine, as well as beforehand, to maintain your flexibility before you can add more intense abdominal exercises or increase frequency.

You can help keep your hip flexors stretched with certain everyday activities. Take the stairs down rather than the elevator; not only will you keep your muscles supple, you will burn more calories.

If you find yourself extremely inflexible and want to enhance your overall flexibility, I strongly recommend you pick up *The BackSmart Fitness Plan*. You'll find plenty of stretches to help you improve your range of motion in all your muscle groups, and you'll be more focused on exercising your midsection rather than fighting tight muscle groups.

CHAPTER SUMMARY

- The iliopsoas muscle group becomes chronically tight with our modern lifestyles.
- We need to stretch out our hip flexors daily to maintain the optimum range of motion in this region.
- By eliminating the stiffness in the hip flexors, you can focus on the abdominal region and other core movements.
- Stretching this region will pay dividends by preventing injuries to this region, enhancing your flexibility, and stretching your abdominal wall.

PART 2

Your Workout: Ultimate Core Fitness

CHAPTER 4

ALTERNATIVE MOVES TO BUILD A STRONGER, FIRMER MIDSECTION

Many of life's everyday activities involve rounding your body forward, whether you're picking up your children, putting dishes in the dishwasher, tossing laundry in the dryer, working at your computer, or simply driving. When you consider how much time you spend doing these repetitive tasks, it's no wonder so many people are walking around with rounded shoulders and slouching posture, not to mention the aches and pains associated with this body position. Walking all day in a slump weakens and tightens your postural muscles, including your hip flexors, compressing your rib cage and diaphragm, as well as weakening your abdominal muscles and lower back region.

Performing the same workouts in the same way over and over again will also create a muscle imbalance, resulting in tight hip flexors as we discussed in the previous chapter. And if your posture when exercising is poor, it will lead to aches and pains and set you up for injuries. Because your body works as a unit, muscle imbalance is often a result of how you move your body, as I explained while discussing the typical crunch exercise that people do today. If you don't balance out these muscle imbalances, exercising can result in all kinds of aches and pains.

Fortunately, you can counteract this rounding forward and compressing by stretching your postural muscles including your psoas (hip flexors) and by centering your workout with functional core movements that give you dynamic angles of movement, rather than short, static exercises (like the basic crunch). Focusing on your deeper core trunk-stabilizing muscles as a unit will enhance your appearance; you will be standing up straighter, and your abs will be tighter and stronger. Your core strength is your ticket to an amazing midsection and provides you with more vibrant health and vitality. Incorporating all of this chapter's functional exercises into your routine is beneficial, because the stronger your core strength is, the better your body will work overall.

Advanced Froggies

This movement is similar to the frog kick in the water.

Muscles emphasized: Lower abdominals

1. Sit on the floor or on a bench. Keep your legs straight in front of you with a slight bend in your knees, and rest your hands gently on your knees.

4.1a
Advanced
Froggies

2. Lift your legs off the floor with your abdominal muscles, focusing on the lower abs.

3. Using your lower abdominals, slowly bend your knees and bring your feet inward toward your body.

4. Hold for 2 seconds, extend your legs again, and repeat step 3.

5. After 6 repetitions, place your hands out to the sides and hold them there for another 6 repetitions of steps 3 and 4.

6. For a more advanced movement, stretch your arms overhead and hold them there for an additional 6 repetitions of steps 3 and 4.

Key Points to Remember

- Try not to rest your feet on the floor between repetitions.

- Do not lean back too far past 45 degrees, as doing so will place stress on your lower back and turn the exercise mainly into a hip flexor movement rather than a lower-abdominal movement.

Elevated Quarter-Turn Jackknives

Muscles emphasized: Upper and lower abdominals and obliques

1. Rest on your right side with your right forearm on the floor at shoulder level and your left arm stretched toward the ceiling. Your legs are outstretched with a slight bend at your knees, and your feet should be together.

2. Inhale as you raise your legs together. Bring them up toward your side as high as you can.

3. Squeeze your abdominals as you lower your left arm and touch your ankle. Hold for 2 seconds, and then lower your legs back to the beginning position. Repeat the movement.

4.2a
Elevated
Quarter-Turn
Jackknives

4.2b
Elevated
Quarter-Turn
Jackknives

Alternative Version

If you are unable to perform this movement with straight legs, bend your
knees, bringing your legs closer to your waistline before starting the exercise. As you raise your bent legs, bring the elbow of your top arm across
your body down toward your bottom knee.

Key Points to Remember

- Do not swing your legs up, turning this into a hip exercise.

- Try to lift your legs as high as you can to stimulate your entire abdominal
  region.

Can Opener

Muscles emphasized: Upper and lower abdominals

1. Lie on your back with your knees bent and feet flat on the floor.

2. Place the outside of one foot onto the opposite knee. Maintain this foot position throughout the movement.

3. Place your hands behind your head, and slowly curl your upper body toward your knees, simultaneously bringing your knees toward the center of your body.

4.3a Can Opener

4. Hold at the top for 2 seconds. Lower to the starting position and repeat.

5. Switch leg position to the other side, and repeat the exercise.

4.3b   Can Opener

Advanced Can Opener with Leg Raised

Muscles emphasized: Upper and lower abdominals

1. Begin by lying on your back with your knees bent and your feet together flat on the floor. Place your hands behind your head.

2. Cross your left leg over your right leg, resting your left ankle on your right knee.

3. Raise your upper body as you raise your right foot, bringing your knees in toward your elbows.

4. Contract and hold for 2 seconds. Lower your upper and lower torso to the start position, but do not rest your feet on the ground.

5. Complete a set, and then repeat on the opposite side.

Advanced Movement

As you become stronger, raise your straight leg higher, and keep it above knee level throughout the entire set before switching to the opposite side.

4.4a, b
Advanced
Can Opener
with Leg
Raised

Key Points to Remember

- Focus on lifting your knee up and toward your elbows during the movement. Concentrate on contracting your abdominal muscles during the entire activity, not just at the beginning of the movement.

- Don't hold your breath when performing this movement; that will only limit your range of motion.

- Do not use momentum to get you through the exercise. Concentrate on working the entire midsection during each phase of the movement.

Cross-Over Crunches

Muscles emphasized: Lower abdominals and obliques

1. Begin by lying on your back with your knees bent at a 90-degree angle and your feet together above the floor. Place your hands behind your head.

2. Raise your upper torso toward one side of your body as you bring your knees up together toward the opposite side of your upper body.

4.5a
Cross-Over
Crunches

4.5b
Cross-Over
Crunches

3. Contract and hold for 3 seconds. Return to the start position without resting your feet on the ground.

4. Repeat to the opposite side, alternating back and forth during the set until you have completed the set.

Key Points to Remember

- Focus on turning your knee up and toward your armpit during the movement.

- Concentrate on contracting all your lower abdominal muscles during the activity, not just at the beginning of the movement.

- Don't hold your breath when performing this movement; that will only limit your range of motion.

- Do not use momentum to get you through the exercise. Instead, concentrate on working the entire midsection during each phase of the movement.

- Remember to raise your upper body up and over toward your hips. Don't just move to the side of your body; that common mistake will rob you of stimulating the entire region.

Alternating Double Ankle Touches

Muscles emphasized: Upper abdominals and obliques

1. Lie on your back with your legs straight and your feet pointing toward the ceiling. Your arms are outstretched over your head and resting on the floor.

2. Pull in your abdominals as you raise both your hands off the floor, placing them on your left ankle. Hold for 1 second, and then come halfway down. Cross over toward your right ankle. Hold for 1 second, and return to the start position.

4.6a, b
Alternating Double Ankle Touches

4.6c
Alternating
Double Ankle
Touches

Key Points to Remember

- Don't jerk yourself up during the movement.

- Focus on feeling all your muscle groups working.

- Concentrate on contracting all your lower abdominal muscles at the top of the motion.

- Don't hold your breath when performing this movement; that will only limit your range of motion.

- Do not turn this movement into an upper-arm exercise by emphasizing your arms swinging up.

- Do not lead with your head by lifting it faster than your arms.

What sets the next exercises apart from a typical crunch movement is that you try to raise yourself as high as you can without activating your stronger hip flexors, as we discussed in the previous chapter. Remember not to jerk yourself up into the positions. Instead, contract and use your abdominal muscles during the entire movements.

Two-Inch Crunch

The two-inch crunch is for old-school exercise enthusiasts who need some form of a crunch in their workouts. The difference is that you'll activate your lower as well as your upper abdominals during the movement.

Muscles emphasized: Upper and lower abdominals

1. Lie on your back with your knees bent and feet flat on the floor.

2. Without lifting your head and while keeping your knees together, raise your feet about 2 to 3 inches above the floor. Hold this foot position throughout the movement.

3. Place your hands behind your head, and slowly curl up.

4. Hold at the top for 2 seconds, and then lower to the starting position; repeat.

4.7a
Two-Inch
Crunch

4.7b
Two-Inch
Crunch

Alternative Version

By raising and lowering your feet, you can increase and decrease the intensity of the movement. To decrease resistance, raise your feet higher to flatten your lower back and place less emphasis on the lower abdominal muscles. To increase resistance, bring your feet closer to the floor. If you feel neck or back tension or soreness, curl your legs up and rest your hands on your knees in front of you to release tension.

Key Points to Remember

- Do not bend your knees toward your chest; keep them at 90 degrees with your hips.

- To isolate your abdominals, contract your abdominal muscles strongly at the top of the movement.

- Execute this movement slowly; a bad habit is to rush through this exercise.

The following exercises are more functional and deeper core movements that not only work the abdominal region but focus on using all your body parts to work as a unit, thus providing greater stimulation to the midsection and surrounding muscle groups.

Straight-Leg Bicycles

Muscles emphasized: Lower and upper abdominals and obliques

1. Begin by lying on your back with your knees bent and your feet together. Place your hands behind your head.

2. Straighten your legs by raising your feet toward the ceiling.

4.8a
Straight-Leg
Bicycles

4.8b
Straight-Leg
Bicycles

3. Bring your right leg down toward the floor without touching the floor. At the same time, cross your right elbow toward your left leg.

4. Contract your abdominal muscles and hold for 1 second. Switch sides by raising your right leg straight up and holding it there while you lower your left leg and move your left elbow toward your right leg.

5. Repeat steps 3 and 4, scissoring your legs while you touch your legs with alternating elbows until you have completed the set.

Key Points to Remember

- Focus on bringing your legs up to 90 degrees and bringing them down for the second half of the movement.

- Concentrate on contracting your abdominal muscles during the entire activity, especially at the beginning of the movement.

- Don't hold your breath when performing this movement; that will only limit your range of motion.

- Do not whip your legs back and forth for the duration of the movement, turning it into a leg exercise.

- Remember to raise your upper body as far as you can while touching your knees.

- If you feel a strain in your lower back or feel your midsection fatigues too quickly, do this movement with bent knees.

Leg Presses

Muscles emphasized: Lower and upper abdominals

1. Begin by lying on your back with your knees bent and your feet together on the floor. Place your outstretched arms above and in front of your hips.

2. Bend your leg, pulling your left knee toward your chest. Hold this position as you raise your upper body slightly off the floor.

4.9a
Leg Presses

4.9b
Leg Presses

4.9c
Leg Presses

3. Bring your arms up and forward as you press your left leg out straight in front of you. As you move, try to reach for your left foot with your hands.

4. Contract and hold for 2 seconds. Return to the starting position, switch legs, and repeat the movement, alternating sides throughout the set.

Key Points to Remember

- Focus on pushing your leg forward, rather than just bringing it along. Really contract all your muscles during the movement.

- Concentrate on contracting your abdominal muscles.

- Do not use momentum to get you through the exercise; concentrate on working the entire midsection during each phase of the movement.

- Remember to raise your upper body as far as you can while trying to touch your foot.

Double-Knee Pull-Ins

Muscles emphasized: Lower and upper abdominals

1. Begin in the push-up position, resting on top of your feet, or alternative plank position. Rest on your forearms depending on your strength. Keep your knees straight and your feet together.

2. Bend at your knees, pulling your legs forward toward your chest.

4.10a
Double-Knee
Pull-Ins

3. Contract and hold for 2 seconds. Pushing your legs back, return the start position.

4. After a few repetitions, start to move your legs faster, and squeeze at the top of the movement before returning to the beginning position.

Key Points to Remember

- Focus on bringing your legs up to your chest and holding this position briefly before you return to the start position.

- Concentrate on contracting your abdominal muscles during the entire activity.

- Don't hold your breath when performing this movement.

- Do not raise your hips too high in the air; rather, force yourself to keep your back as straight as possible.

- A secondary benefit of the movement is that it will help build a strong core and arm and chest muscles.

4.10b
Double-Knee
Pull-Ins

Crisscross Leg Pull-Ins

Muscles emphasized: Lower abdominals and obliques

If you are not strong enough to remain in the push-up or plank position for all the repetitions, drop to your knees to complete this exercise. As with the double-knee pull-ins, try not to turn this exercise into merely an upper-body workout. Focus on your core, and pull your knees in as far and as high as possible for that deep, strong contraction of the abdominal muscles.

1. Start in the push-up position with your feet together. If you don't feel strong enough at this time for this position, you can start by resting on your forearms in the plank position.

2. Slowly squeeze your abdominals in as you slowly bend your right knee and pull it in toward the left side of your chest. Hold this position for 2 seconds.

3. Slowly relax the contraction of your leg and hip muscles as you place your foot back in the start position. Repeat with the same leg until you complete the set. Then move on to the opposite side.

4.11a
Crisscross
Leg Pull-Ins

4.11b
Crisscross
Leg Pull-Ins

Advanced Movement

To increase the intensity, increase the distance between your feet at the beginning of the exercise. This will further challenge your core.

Key Points to Remember

- Don't race through the movement. Focus on feeling all your muscle groups working.

- Concentrate on contracting all your muscles at the end range of motion and then relaxing as you return to the start position.

- Don't hold your breath when performing this movement; that will only limit your range of motion as a result of tight diaphragm muscles.

- Do not turn this movement into an upper-body exercise by just resting your weight on your arms.

- Remember to start the movement by contracting your abdominals before you start to pull your knee in and up as far as possible.

Super Abs

Muscles emphasized: Lower and upper abdominals

1. Begin by lying on your back with your legs straight and your feet together pointing up at the ceiling. Place your arms outstretched over your head and resting on the floor.

2. Raise your upper body, and touch your ankles with your hands. Hold for 2 seconds while contracting your abdominals. Lower your upper body and arms to the start position.

3. Lower your legs to about 45 degrees from the floor with a slight bend in your knees. Hold for 2 seconds, and then return them to the start position with your feet pointing toward the ceiling.

4. Bring your straight legs toward your chest, and if you can, lift your lower body and continue moving your feet to the floor above your head. Slowly raise your legs back to the start position. Repeat steps 2 to 4 until you have completed the set.

4.12a
Super Abs

4.12b
Super Abs

4.12c
Super Abs

Key Points to Remember

- Focus on bringing your legs up to 90 degrees and holding this position during the first half of the movement.

- Make sure you are careful when lowering your legs; don't just drop them down. Use your abdominal muscles.

- If you are unable to touch the floor behind you, then bend your knees as close to your chest as possible to get a deep contraction of your lower abdominal muscles.

- Concentrate on contracting your abdominal muscles during the entire activity, not just at the beginning of the movement.

- Don't hold your breath when performing this movement; that will only limit your range of motion.

- Do not use momentum to get through the exercise. Instead, concentrate on working the entire midsection during each phase of the movement.

- Remember to raise your upper body as far as you can while touching your ankles.

Elevated Butterflies

Muscles emphasized: Lower and upper abdominals

1. Begin by lying on your back with your knees bent out to the sides and your feet together with the soles against each other. Raise your feet together 2 to 3 inches off the ground. Place your hands behind your head.

4.13a
Elevated
Butterflies

4.13b
Elevated
Butterflies

2. Raise your upper body, and curl toward your knees, reaching with the elbows toward your knees.

3. Contract and hold for 2 seconds. Return to the start position.

Key Points to Remember

- Focus on holding your feet together and keeping your legs relaxed throughout the movement.

- Concentrate on pulling in your abdominal muscles at the beginning of the movement.

- Don't hold your breath when performing this movement; that will only limit your range of motion.

- Keep your back flat during the duration of the exercise.

- Raise your upper body as far as you can while trying to touch your knees with your elbows.

- If you feel your back arching too much, then lower your feet until your back becomes flat again.

CHAPTER SUMMARY

By doing these exercises as part of the AbSmart system, you will learn to realign your hips, shoulders, and spine while correcting postural problems and strengthening any weak links related to your core. Each progression of exercises allows you to focus on building and strengthening those core muscles and tightening your midsection from all sides. To intensify your workouts and make them more efficient, you can incorporate more core muscles each time you perform the movements over the next few weeks. You'll feel the difference as you get stronger and more in control of your body.

Adding leg movements improves your leg and hip flexibility while strengthening your shoulders and trunk muscles.

Now it's time to move on to more exercises, which will improve your coordination and tighten your waistline.

CHAPTER 5

NEW TWISTS FOR SCULPTING YOUR LOVE HANDLES

In the gym and in exercise classes, hardly anyone performs the moves described in this chapter. Instead, people focus on crunches. That's unfortunate, because incorporating these moves could put exercisers further ahead (just as you will be) in the game of controlling and strengthening their waistlines.

These exercises will firm and sculpt your midsection with fun and effective movements. They do not torque or compress the spine, as those old-fashioned twists with the bar across your shoulders do. All these moves focus on the intercostals and obliques (love handles), which most people tend to exercise as a second thought or ignore altogether.

If you put your energy into these exercises, your waistline will become tighter, and you'll be on your way to obtaining that tapered look to your torso. You'll also strengthen your all-important core muscles and improve flexibility in this region by emphasizing your muscle alignment to sculpt and tone your midsection while preventing injury.

Elevated Corkscrews

Muscles emphasized: Lower abdominals and obliques

1. Begin by lying on your back with your arms by your sides.

2. Inhale as you slowly raise your legs 90 degrees.

3. Exhale as you contract your abdominals, and turn your legs slightly toward the right. Hold for 2 seconds, and then lower to the start position.

4. Immediately raise your legs and turn to the opposite side. Hold for 2 seconds, and then return to the start position. Repeat the entire movement.

5.1a
Elevated
Corkscrews

5.1b
Elevated
Corkscrews

Key Points to Remember

- Focus on bringing your legs up, turning them to the side, and holding this position briefly before returning to the start position.

- Concentrate on contracting your abdominal muscles at the top of the movement.

- Do not use momentum to get you through the exercise.

- Do not throw your hips up in the air; instead, force yourself to focus on your core for strength.

Seated Bicycle Rotations

Muscles emphasized: Lower and upper abdominals and obliques

1. Begin by sitting with your hands behind your head and your knees bent with your feet close together and flat on the floor, while leaning back slightly.

2. Inhale as you raise your feet off the floor with your knees bent until your feet are above your knee height.

3. Exhale as you contract your abdominals as you bring your left leg toward your left shoulder and simultaneously bring your right elbow toward your left knee.

5.2a
Seated
Bicycle Rotations

5.2b
Seated
Bicycle Rotations

4. Point your left elbow behind you as far as possible while you are exhaling. Hold for 2 seconds. Return to the start position. Repeat with the opposite leg and elbow.

5. Alternatively, you can keep your arms out to the sides and rotate your arms back and forth rather than touching your elbows to your knees.

Key Points to Remember

• Focus on trying to bring your feet up and above your knee height throughout the entire movement.

• Concentrate on contracting your abdominal muscles at the top of the movement when your elbow touches your knee.

• Do not twist your waistline when performing the exercise. Rather, focus on your muscles turning your torso through the movement.

• When you turn your torso, point the elbow not touching your knee as far behind you as you can.

Side Arm Squeezes

Muscles emphasized: Upper abdominals and obliques

1. Begin by lying on your back with your hands resting by your sides. Bend your knees, and place your feet together flat on the floor.

2. Exhale as you raise your feet off the floor with your knees bent until your feet are above your knee height.

3. Place your straight left arm across your torso, stretched toward your right hip. Grasp your left hand with your right, and hold your hands together by your right side of your body.

4. Contract your abdominals as you bring your knees up and toward your left shoulder, simultaneously pulling your hands down toward your hip on the opposite side. Make sure to lift your shoulders off the floor during this part of the exercise to get a complete contraction.

5. Hold for 2 seconds. Return to the start position. Repeat on the opposite side, holding your hands on the left side of your body.

5.3a
Side Arm
Squeezes

5.3b
Side Arm
Squeezes

Key Points to Remember

- Focus on bringing your feet up and above your knee height throughout the entire movement.

- Concentrate on contracting your abdominal muscles during the entire activity.

- Do not twist your waistline when performing the exercise. Rather, focus on your core muscles turning your torso through the movement.

- Lift your shoulders as you contract your abdominal muscles during the movement.

Arm Circles

Muscles emphasized: Upper abdominals and obliques

1. Begin by lying on your back with your hands resting together on your midsection. Bend your knees, and place your feet together flat on the floor.

2. Contract your abdominals before starting the arm movement.

3. Stretch your arms straight up over your head, and move them together in a clockwise circle (parallel to the floor), raising your shoulders and head off the floor during the duration of the exercise. Move all the way around the circle until you return to the start position.

5.4a
Arm Circles

5.4b
Arm Circles

5.4c
Arm Circles

5.4d
Arm Circles

4. After completing your repetitions in one direction, without resting move your arms counterclockwise until the set is complete.

5. Breathe deeply throughout the movement.

Key Points to Remember

• Focus on bringing your head and shoulders up far enough to feel the upper and lower abdominals engaged in the exercise.

• Concentrate on contracting your abdominal muscles during the entire activity.

• Do not pull with the arms; rather, use them as resistance and a guide right through the movement.

Side-Turning Ankle Touches

Muscles emphasized: Upper abdominals and obliques

1. Begin by lying on your back with your arms resting out to your sides at shoulder height. Bend your knees, and place your feet flat on the floor.

2. Contract your abdominals as you raise your feet until they are slightly above your knees.

3. Move your knees together toward the floor on your right side, contracting your oblique muscles, and stop at about 45 degrees.

4. Raise your feet forward from this position, keeping a slight bend in your knees. At the same time, raise your left hand and stretch it toward your legs, touching your right ankle. Hold for 2 seconds.

5. After completing your repetitions in one direction, without resting repeat in the opposite direction until the set is complete.

6. Breathe deeply throughout the movement.

5.5a, b Side-Turning Ankle Touches

Key Points to Remember

- Focus on keeping your knees together at the beginning of the movement to ensure complete activation of all the abdominal muscle groups.

- Try to touch your ankle and hold that position for at least 2 seconds before lowering your upper body toward the opposite side.

- Concentrate on contracting your abdominal muscles during the entire exercise.

- Do not pull with the arms; rather, use them as resistance and a guide right through the movement.

Sideways Elbow-to-Leg Touches

Muscles emphasized: Lower abdominals and obliques

1. Begin by lying on your left side with your head resting on your left hand for support. Your legs are together in line with your body and with a slight bend in the knees.

2. Contract your abdominals as you raise your legs while bringing your right elbow toward your legs and touching them if you can. Hold this position for 2 seconds, contracting your obliques. Return to the start position.

3. Complete the number of repetitions on one side, and then switch to the other side.

5.6a
Sideways
Elbow-to-Leg
Touches

5.6b
Sideways
Elbow-to-Leg
Touches

Key Points to Remember

- Focus on bringing your legs and elbow together at the top of the movement to ensure complete activation of all your abdominal muscle groups.

- Try to touch and hold that position for at least 2 seconds before lowering your legs. Try not to rest your legs at the bottom of the movement before bringing them back up.

- Concentrate on contracting your abdominal muscles during the entire activity.

HOW EFFICIENT IS YOUR TRAINING?

The next set of exercises will show you whether you are training efficiently or not and how to make sure you are training your core at your best. Since the AbSmart system is a holistic approach, you may find it runs counter to certain standard principles of athletic, sports, or abdominal training that you've learned or seen at the gym. The truth is, these traditional training regimens are often counterproductive. Although sports scientists have undertaken research that condemns many training myths, exercises based on those myths are still used in many gyms and workouts, resulting in less efficient training.

One training principle that seems to be consistently beaten to death by people who train their midsections is the principle of specificity. The principle of specificity states one must mimic as closely as possible conditions and variables of the muscles being exercised in order to maximize learning and training effects. In contrast, when you use the AbSmart system, your training will duplicate the biomechanics, neuromuscular patterns, and energy system requirements to stabilize your entire core region rather than just one plane of movement. In other words, let yourself explore your range of motion, and go outside your comfort zone. Reach a little bit farther or hold the positions a tad longer to improve your body's shape.

Side Elbow Bridges

Muscles emphasized: Upper abdominals and obliques

1. Begin by lying on your left side while resting on your left forearm at shoulder height. Rest your legs on the floor in alignment with your body.

2. Place your right hand behind your head with your elbow pointing up toward the ceiling.

5.7a
Side Elbow Bridges

5.7b
Side Elbow
Bridges

3. Raise your body up from your waist as you contract your abdominal muscles, and hold yourself up in this position.

4. Bring your right elbow down and in front of your chest, trying to touch your elbow to the floor. Contract your midsection, and hold for 2 seconds before returning to the step 3 position, still holding yourself up.

5. After completing your repetitions on one side, without resting repeat on the opposite side until the set is complete.

6. Breathe deeply throughout the movement.

Key Points to Remember

- Focus on turning with your midsection, rather than just pulling your elbow down toward the floor during the movement. This ensures complete activation of your oblique muscles.

- Try to hold yourself up without bending at your waist or relaxing your lower back muscles when performing this exercise.

- Concentrate on contracting your abdominal muscles during the entire exercise.

Side Push-Up Bridges

Muscles emphasized: Upper abdominals and obliques

This is a more advanced version of the previous exercise. Before you progress to this exercise, make sure you can perform side elbow bridges equally well on both sides of your body.

1. Begin by lying on your left side while resting on your left forearm at shoulder height, with straight legs resting on the floor.

2. Raise your right arm straight up toward the ceiling.

3. Raise your body by pushing with your left hand until your left arm is completely straight as you contract your abdominal muscles, and hold yourself up in this position.

5.8a
Side Push-Up
Bridges

5.8b
Side Push-Up
Bridges

4. Bring your right elbow down in front of your chest, and try to touch your elbow to the floor. Contract your midsection, and hold for 2 seconds. Return to the step 3 position, still holding yourself up. (If this is too difficult to perform at first, keep your right arm straight, and touch the floor with your right hand instead of your elbow until your balance and strength become sufficient.)

5. After completing your repetitions on one side, without resting repeat on the opposite side until the set is complete.

6. Breathe deeply throughout the movement.

Key Points to Remember

• Focus on turning with your midsection, rather than just pulling your arms down toward the floor during the movement. This ensures complete activation of your oblique muscles.

• Try to hold yourself up without bending at your waist or relaxing your lower back muscles when performing this exercise.

• Concentrate on balancing with your core, rather than just your arm strength.

Side Bridges with Knee Raises

Muscles emphasized: Lower abdominals and obliques

This again is a more advanced movement. Women may actually find this exercise easier than the side push-up bridges because they typically have a lower center of gravity then men. Make sure you maintain good form when performing this and the other exercises in this chapter for developing a stronger, firmer waistline.

1. Begin by lying on your left side while resting on your left forearm at shoulder height. Your legs should be slightly bent at the knees and resting on the floor.

2. Place your right hand in front of you for balance at the beginning. As you advance, rest it on your hip for added resistance and balance control.

3. Raise your body by lifting your hips off the floor while contracting your midsection until your legs are completely straight. Hold yourself up in this position.

4. Pull your bottom knee in toward your chest. Hold for 2 seconds. Lower your leg to the step 3 position, and then repeat the entire movement.

5.9a
Side Bridges with
Knee Raises

5.9b
Side Bridges with
Knee Raises

5. After completing your repetitions on one side, without resting repeat the exercise on the opposite side until the set is complete.

6. Breathe deeply throughout the movement.

Key Points to Remember

- Focus on keeping your balance while performing the movement.

- Try to hold yourself up without bending at your waist or relaxing your lower back muscles.

- Concentrate on balancing with your core rather than just your arm strength during the movement.

- Bring your knee as close as you can with your abdominal muscles, rather than swinging your leg up.

Pocket Reaches

Muscles emphasized: Upper abdominals and obliques

1. Begin by lying on your back with your hands resting by your sides and your elbows slightly bent. Bend your knees, and place your feet flat on the floor.

2. Raise your upper body to lift your shoulders off the floor.

3. Keeping your shoulders off the floor, reach your left hand toward your left ankle or farther, bending at the waist. Hold for 2 seconds, and return to the step 2 position.

4. In the same way, reach your right hand on the right side of your body.

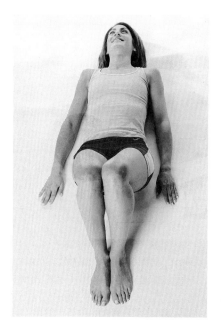

5.10a, b
Pocket Reaches

5.10c
Pocket Reaches

5. Alternate sides during the set.

6. Breathe deeply throughout the movement.

Key Points to Remember

- Focus on keeping your shoulders elevated during the entire exercise.

- Concentrate on contracting your obliques along the sides of your waist-line while performing the movement.

Seated Torsal Rotation

Muscles emphasized: Lower and upper abdominals and obliques

1. Sit up tall, bending your knees slightly and placing your feet flat on the ground next to each other. Do not round your back forward, compressing down onto your core; rather, try to sit tall and straight with your abdominal muscles pulled in.

2. Exhale as you begin turning your midsection toward your right while leaning back 35 to 45 degrees. Not sure when you have the correct angle? For an easier time with the exercises, lean back slightly off center. It is harder right between falling back onto your back and halfway sitting up—"the sticking point."

3. After rotating to the right as comfortably as you can, slowly move toward the center and rotate toward your left. Then move forward until

5.11a, b Seated Torsal Rotation

5.11c
Seated
Torsal
Rotation

you are sitting up, remembering to raise your back to a straight position. Repeat this step.

4. After completing your repetitions, change directions.

Seated Froggy with Arm Rotation

Muscles emphasized: Lower abdominals and obliques

1. Start by sitting with your knees bent and your feet flat on the floor. Raise your arms in front of your body at shoulder height.

2. Pull your knees in toward your chest, keeping your arms out in front of you at eye level.

5.12a
Seated Froggy with
Arm Rotation

5.12b
Seated Froggy with
Arm Rotation

3. Straighten your legs in front of you at 45 degrees. As you do so, rotate at your midsection to the right, moving your arms out to the side and behind you as far as they will go while maintaining your arms straight and hands at shoulder or waist height throughout the movement.

4. Pull in your knees toward your chest, and return your arms forward at shoulder height.

5. Repeat the movement to the left side as you straighten your legs.

6. You can keep one leg bent or keep one foot on the floor at first until you build strength, flexibility, and stability.

Hip Turns with Crunch

Muscles emphasized: Lower and upper abdominals and obliques

1. Begin by lying on your back with your hands resting behind your head. Bend your knees, and place your feet flat on the floor, touching each other.

5.13a
Hip Turns
with Crunch

2. Keeping your knees together, bend them to one side as far as you can go. From here, raise your feet so they are about 2 to 3 inches off the floor. Keep this position throughout the exercise.

3. Raise your upper body, lifting your shoulders off the floor. Hold in the top position for 2 seconds, and then return to the step 2 position. After completing your repetitions on one side, repeat the entire exercise on the opposite side.

Key Points to Remember

• Keep your hips and shoulders squared. Don't allow them to roll.

• Keep your neck straight.

5.13b
Hip Turns
with Crunch

Swiss Ball Turns

Muscles emphasized: Lower abdominals and obliques

1. Start by lying on the floor on your stomach. Place your feet on the ball with your legs straight, keeping your spine aligned as you raise yourself up into a push-up position. Make sure you are looking down at the floor, balancing with your feet on the ball. You can use a chair if you do not have a ball.

2. Exhale as you pull in your abdominal muscles, focusing on controlling the ball so there is very little movement. Then slowly turn yourself sideways, leaving one foot on the ball and raising the opposite foot off the ball as far as you can go. Hold the top position for 2 seconds, and then return your foot to the ball. Repeat with the opposite leg, alternating legs throughout your set.

Key Points to Remember

- At the beginning, focus on controlling the ball's movement. Keep from listing to one side as you raise your opposite leg during the exercise.

- Hold in your abdominal muscles throughout the exercise, maintaining a solid core. This will maintain proper spinal alignment and strengthen your lower back muscles at the same time.

5.14a
Swiss
Ball Turns

5.14b
Swiss
Ball Turns

As you can see from this chapter of exercises, not only are you building a stronger foundation toward a rock-hard midsection, you also are improving your core muscle control and stamina. That will help you throughout your daily activities and in playing sports.

The bonus is you don't even need a gym membership to do these exercises. They all can be done anywhere with the minimum amount of time and space.

Now that you have worked your sides, let's move on in your journey toward a stronger, firmer midsection by hitting the lower core—an often neglected but truly important section, not to be overlooked or undertrained.

CHAPTER 6

SHRINK YOUR WAISTLINE WITH LOWER-CORE POWER

Most people who work their midsection focus on what they can see, avoiding the parts they would rather not look at. This chapter is for those people. Focusing on the area right below the belt line from the front and back will greatly enhance your shape and reduce the dimension of your girth in this region. This is the location where the belt becomes looser or we try to cover up by wearing our shirt untucked. If you follow a few simple guidelines, you will be proudly tucking in again, with a slimmer, stronger lower core beneath your shirt.

TIPS FOR SUCCESS

It's important to remember, first of all, to avoid any form of quick movements driven more by momentum than the muscles in the area. Second, stop the exercise before you completely fatigue your muscles. It will not do you any good to reach complete muscle failure with these exercises; doing so will cause you to lose form and possibly injure yourself by overexerting. Third, as you progress and become stronger, go ahead and add more variety to your exercises by increasing the number of repetitions or adding resistance when appropriate.

Finally, stick with it! When you create a stronger foundation, you will feel and see the results with each new workout session. These moves not only strengthen your abdominals against gravity, but they also challenge your body as a fully integrated unit. To keep stable during the motions, you'll be using almost all the muscles in your body—back muscles, glutes, legs, the important pelvic floor muscles, and lower abdominals.

Body Weight Planks

Muscles emphasized: Spinal erectors, glutes, lower and upper abdominals

1. Start by lying on the floor on your stomach with your legs outstretched and your feet on the floor. Rest on your forearms with your elbows directly under your shoulders with your hands flat on the floor. Make sure your elbows are not too far forward of your shoulders, for this will put too much stress on your joints and will make the exercise much harder.

2. Exhale as you pull in your abdominal muscles, focusing on the lower region being pulled in. (Imagine trying to touch your spine with your abdominal muscles.)

3. Raise your legs until they are straight and you are looking down at the floor, balancing on your toes and forearms.

4. Hold the top position for 15 seconds. (As you grow stronger, build up to 1 minute.) Slowly lower back down while inhaling. When your knees touch the floor, exhale and return to the upright position for another round of holding.

6.1
Body Weight Planks

Dumbbell Raise Planks

Muscles emphasized: Spinal erectors, glutes, lower and upper abdominals

1. Start by placing a dumbbell between your knees while kneeling. Reach forward into the plank position, resting on your forearms with your elbows directly under your shoulders and your feet resting on the floor. Make sure your elbows are not too far forward of your shoulders, for this will put too much stress on your joints and will make the exercise much harder.

2. Squeeze the dumbbell in place between your knees as you raise your legs up until they are straight and you are looking down at the floor, balancing on your toes and forearms.

3. Exhale as you pull in your abdominal muscles, focusing on the lower region being pulled in. (Imagine trying to touch your spine with your abdominal muscles.)

4. Hold the top position for 5 seconds, gradually building up to 30 seconds or longer.

5. Inhale as you lower yourself until your knees touch the floor. Exhale and return to the upright position for another round.

6.2
Dumbbell
Raise Planks

Key Points to Remember

- Use a light-enough weight that you can at least complete 3 sets of 5-second holding positions. If you are unable to hold for this long, do not use any extra weight but just your own body weight.

- Make sure to hold in your abdominal muscles throughout the exercise, maintaining a solid core. This will maintain proper spinal alignment and strengthen your lower back muscles at the same time.

- Make sure to maintain a neutral spine while holding the weight in place; this will help stimulate the deep core muscles.

- Squeeze your glutes as you come up and hold the top position. Do not relax them in the upright position.

Plank Wide Leg Raises

Muscles emphasized: Spinal erectors, glutes, and lower abdominals

1. Start by lying on the floor on your stomach with your legs outstretched and your feet on the floor. Your elbows should be aligned directly under your shoulders with your hands flat on the floor shoulder-width apart. Make sure your elbows are not too far forward of your shoulders, for this will put too much stress on your joints and will make the exercise much harder.

2. Raise your legs until they are straight and you are looking down at the floor, balancing on your toes and forearms.

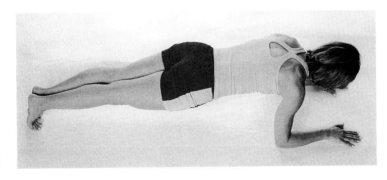

6.3a
Plank Wide
Leg Raises

6.3b
Plank Wide
Leg Raises

3. Exhale as you pull in your abdominal muscles, focusing on the lower region being pulled in. (Imagine trying to touch your spine with your abdominal muscles.)

4. While holding the top position, raise your right leg up and out to the side at hip height or higher. Hold for 2 seconds, gradually building up to 10 seconds or longer. Slowly lower your leg, and then repeat with your left leg for the same number of seconds.

5. Inhale as you touch your knees to the floor. Exhale and return to the upright position for another round of leg raises.

Key Points to Remember

- If you are unable to hold your leg up while it is out to the side, you can raise it in the center position or bring it out to the side without raising your leg until you are able to perform the movement in its entirety.

- Make sure to hold in your abdominal muscles throughout the exercise, maintaining a solid core. This will maintain proper spinal alignment and strengthen your lower back muscles at the same time.

- Make sure to maintain a neutral spine while holding the weight in place; this will help stimulate the deep core muscles.

- Squeeze your glutes as you come up and out to the side during the movement.

Plank Jacks

Muscles emphasized: Spinal erectors, glutes, and lower abdominals

1. Start by lying on the floor on your stomach with your legs outstretched and your feet resting on the floor. Your elbows should be aligned directly under your shoulders with your hands flat on the floor and less than shoulder-width apart. Make sure your elbows are not too far forward of your shoulders, for this will put too much stress on your joints and will make the exercise much harder.

2. Raise your legs until they are straight and you are looking down at the floor, balancing on your forearms and toes with your feet together.

3. Exhale as you pull in your abdominal muscles, focusing on the lower region being pulled in. (Imagine trying to touch your spine with your abdominal muscles.)

4. While holding the top position, spring your feet out to the sides so they are slightly wider than your shoulder width. Hold for 2 seconds, and then spring back to the center so your feet are together. Gradually build up the number of repetitions you perform.

6.4a
Plank Jacks

6.4b
Plank Jacks

Key Points to Remember

- Make sure to hold in your abdominal muscles throughout the exercise, maintaining a solid core. This will maintain a proper spinal alignment and strengthen your lower back muscles at the same time.

- Make sure to maintain a neutral spine; this will help stimulate the deep core muscles.

- Squeeze your glutes as you come up and move your legs out to the sides.

Wide-Arm Planks

Muscles emphasized: Spinal erectors, glutes, lower and upper abdominals

1. Start by lying on the floor on your stomach with your legs outstretched and your feet resting on the floor. Your elbows should be aligned directly under your shoulders with your hands flat on the floor less than shoulder-width apart. Make sure your elbows are not too far forward of your shoulders.

2. Raise your legs until they are straight and you are looking down at the floor, balancing on your toes and forearms.

3. Exhale as you pull in your abdominal muscles, focusing on the lower region being pulled in. (Imagine trying to touch your spine with your abdominal muscles.)

6.5a, b
Wide-Arm
Planks

4. Keeping your elbow bent, slowly move your right arm out to the side about 12 inches. Supporting your body weight in this position will force you to focus more on your core.

5. Hold this position for 15 seconds, gradually building up to 1 minute. Inhaling, slowly move your right arm to the position in step 2. Exhaling, return to the upright position for a round with the left arm. Repeat with alternating arms.

Key Points to Remember

- As you become stronger, you can add weight between your knees during this exercise. Use a light-enough weight that you can at least complete 3 sets of 15-second holding positions. If you are unable to hold for this long, do not use any extra weight but just your own body weight.

- Hold in your abdominal muscles throughout the exercise, maintaining a solid core. This will maintain proper spinal alignment and strengthen your lower back muscles at the same time.

- When using a weight, make sure to squeeze your inner thigh muscles hard to hold the weight in place. This will help stimulate the deep core muscles.

- Squeeze your glutes as you come up and hold the top position. Do not relax them in the upright position.

- Do not attempt to move your arm out more than a few inches when first starting the movement; gradually build up to a wider plank without injuring yourself.

- This exercise is not recommended if you suffer from any type of shoulder problems.

Worm Planks

Muscles emphasized: Spinal erectors, glutes, lower and upper abdominals

1. Start by lying on the floor on your stomach with your legs outstretched and your feet resting on the floor. Your elbows should be aligned directly under your shoulders with your hands shoulder-width apart flat on the floor. Make sure your elbows are not too far forward of your shoulders.

2. Raise your legs until they are straight and you are looking down at the floor, balancing on your toes and forearms.

3. Exhale as you pull in your abdominal muscles, focusing on the lower region being pulled in. (Imagine trying to touch your spine with your abdominal muscles.)

4. Slowly raise your hips toward the ceiling until your legs are at about a 45-degree angle from the floor. Support your body weight in this position for 2 seconds. Lower your hips until your body is parallel with the floor, not touching the floor with your knees. Return to the top position.

6.6a
Worm Planks

6.6b
Worm Planks

6.6c
Worm Planks

6.6d
Worm Planks

6.6e
Worm Planks

5. Return to the parallel position, and turn your hips to face the left as if you were going to take a breath in a freestyle swimming stroke. Hold for 2 seconds, and then roll to your right and hold. Return to the parallel position.

6. Repeat steps 4 and 5, resting only in the parallel position until your set is complete.

Swiss Ball Reverse Leg Raise

Muscles emphasized: Spinal erectors and glutes

1. Start by lying on the floor on your stomach with a Swiss ball near your feet. Place your feet on the ball with your legs straight, keeping your spine aligned as you raise yourself up into a push-up position. Make sure you are looking down at the floor, balancing with your feet on the ball. You can use a chair if you do not have a ball.

2. Exhale as you pull in your abdominal muscles, focusing on controlling the ball so there is very little movement. Slowly raise your leg off the ball a few inches or as high as you can. Hold the top position for 2 seconds, and return your leg to the ball. Repeat with the opposite leg, alternating legs throughout your set.

6.7a
Swiss Ball Reverse
Leg Raise

6.7b
Swiss Ball Reverse
Leg Raise

Key Points to Remember

- At the beginning, focus on controlling the ball movement so it doesn't list to one side as you raise your legs.

- Hold in your abdominal muscles throughout the exercise, maintaining a solid core. This will maintain proper spinal alignment and strengthen your lower back muscles at the same time.

Bench Warmers

Muscles emphasized: Spinal erectors and glutes

1. Begin by sitting on a weighted bench and leaning forward until your waistline is resting on the edge, with your upper body extended off the bench and your arms resting on the floor in the push-up position.

2. Brace your feet under the bench, or have someone hold them against the bench for you.

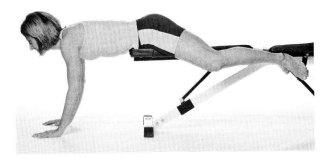

6.8a
Bench Warmers

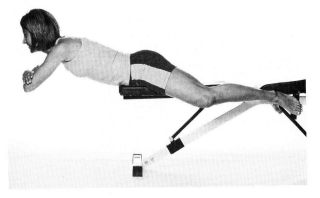

6.8b
Bench Warmers

3. Fold your arms across your chest as you raise your torso until it is parallel with or higher than the top of the bench. Hold for 2 seconds.

4. Slowly bend down to about a 45-degree angle. Hold for 2 seconds, and then raise the back again. Repeat this step.

Key Points to Remember

- Maintain a neutral spine throughout the movement. Do not hyperextend (arch) your back too far upward, nor should you round your back.

- Focus on pulling in your abdominal muscles and contracting your glutes throughout the exercise.

- If you are unable to perform one set, due to lower-back weakness, try the floor exercises for the lower back region in *The BackSmart Fitness Plan* for a month or two. Then return to this exercise and try it again.

Bench Warmers with Swim

Muscles emphasized: Spinal erectors, glutes, and obliques

1. Begin by sitting on a weighted bench so that when you lean forward, your waistline is resting on the edge of the bench with your upper body extended off the bench and your arms resting on the floor in the push-up position.

2. Brace your feet under the bench, or have someone hold them against the bench for you.

6.9a
Bench Warmers
with Swim

6.9b
Bench Warmers
with Swim

6.9c
Bench Warmers
with Swim

3. Bring your arms forward and outstretched to shoulder height. Hold your right arm forward so it is parallel to the floor and in line with your face or higher. Simultaneously bring your left arm parallel to the floor above your hips.

4. Slowly bring your arms to point in the opposite direction as if you are swimming through the air, crossing perpendicular to the floor in one smooth motion and holding the end positions for 2 seconds before repeating.

5. Maintain the body parallel or higher to the floor for as many repetitions as you can. Lower your arms to the floor to rest before starting another set.

Key Points to Remember

- Maintain a neutral spine throughout the movement. Do not hyperextend (arch) your back too far upward, nor should you round your back.

- Focus on pulling in your abdominal muscles and contracting your glutes throughout the exercise.

- Maintain your arm height at face level in front of you and above your hips when bringing your arm back behind while performing the exercise. If you become fatigued, bring your arms down and rest before completing the set. As you get stronger, you'll be able to perform more repetitions.

- If you are unable to perform this movement, return to the bench warmers until you are stronger.

Bench Reverse Leg Raises

Muscles emphasized: Spinal erectors, glutes, and lower abdominals

1. Begin by lying face down on a weighted bench with your hips resting against the edge and toes on the floor.

2. Bring your arms out forward and hold onto the top of the bench with palms down in front of your head.

3. Exhale as you pull in your abdominal muscles and squeeze your glutes as you slowly raise your left leg until it is parallel to the floor or higher. Hold for 2 seconds. Lower your foot back to the floor. Immediately repeat with the opposite leg, alternating until the set is completed.

Advanced Movement

When you become stronger and more stable in your core, slowly raise your right leg and simultaneously raise your left arm to about ear level above the bench. Alternate legs and opposite arms until your set is completed.

6.10a
Bench Reverse
Leg Raises

6.10b
Bench Reverse
Leg Raises

Double-Leg Bench Reverse Raises

Muscles emphasized: Spinal erectors, glutes, and lower abdominals

1. Begin by sitting at the edge of a weighted bench, and then turn around and lie down with your hips resting against the edge of the bench. Rest your toes on the floor.

2. Bring your arms forward and hold onto the bench with hands at face level. Exhale as you pull in your abdominal muscles and squeeze your glutes while slowly raising your legs until they are parallel to the floor. Hold for 2 seconds. Lower your feet back to the floor, and immediately repeat this movement.

6.11a
Double-Leg Bench
Reverse Raises

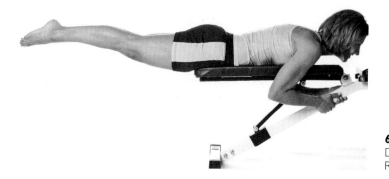

6.11b
Double-Leg Bench
Reverse Raises

One-Arm One-Leg Push-Up Position

Muscles emphasized: Spinal erectors, glutes, lower abdominals, shoulders, and arms

This is an advanced movement (in case you were unable to tell already by the name of the exercise), and it's your last movement in the series of planks. You should try this only when you can hold your own body weight in a push-up position with one arm.

1. Start by getting into a push-up position with your hands and feet placed shoulder-width apart.

2. Raise your right hand out to the side, away from your body, or rest your hand on your lower back.

6.12a
One-Arm One-Leg
Push-Up Position

6.12b
One-Arm One-Leg
Push-Up Position

3. While maintaining this position, slowly raise your right foot above your waistline. Squeeze your glutes as you come up and hold the top position.

4. Hold in your abdominal muscles throughout the exercise, maintaining a solid core. This will maintain proper spinal alignment and strengthen your lower back muscles at the same time.

5. Slowly bend your left arm into a push-up near the floor and then back up.

6. Slowly lower your leg to the floor, and then your arm. Relax all the way down to the floor, and then repeat, using the opposite arm and leg.

Key Points to Remember

- If you find this exercise is too difficult at first, try the following steps to build up to the movement.

- Keep one knee bent on the floor as you raise your opposite leg.

- Raise the opposite leg and arm at the same time to give you more balance.

- Stay on one forearm while performing the movement.

- Do not relax your glutes in the upright position.

Mix up the exercise movements and frequently change directions and angles so you hit your lower abdominals, lower back, glutes, hips, and legs. By doing so, you're actually learning how to use these muscles while getting a harder and stronger midsection. The AbSmart fitness plan is well suited for most women, who may shy away from the gym but still want a well-toned lower core, and for the jock correcting an often common weak link in his or her routine.

Let's move on to adding some resistance to your abdominal routine. The exercises in the next chapter will help you get a flatter midsection.

CHAPTER SUMMARY

As you can see, these exercises run counter to the idea of machine-based workouts—the kind of workouts that isolate a single muscle group. Rather, this functional lower-core program causes you to learn to use multiple muscle groups in an integrated way, synergizing your entire body, challenging your whole body to work collectively in a sequential pattern.

CHAPTER 7

RESISTANCE TRAINING TO BRING OUT YOUR CHISELED ABS

Why would you want to do resistance training for your abs when you are still getting the hang of the other body weight exercises?

There's actually a two-part answer to this question. First, it may be easier for some people to get in a good workout with the added resistance because you will be able to fatigue your abdominal muscles faster than if you hadn't added it. Second, using extra weights may help you become better at the regular weightless exercises. Without getting bogged down in the scientific principles, the short version is that with added weight you are recruiting more muscle fibers while performing the exercise. Increasing the load of your workouts by utilizing a weight barrier that your body as a whole must overcome causes greater muscle gain.

This barrier is also the reason why people who have weak lower back muscles and are excessively out of shape should not attempt to start adding resistance to their workouts until they have built a stronger foundation of core muscles. If you suffer from any back or neck pain, make sure you can do all the other exercises without resistance before increasing your load. Always check with your physician before starting this or any other type of exercise.

With that said, if you are injury-free and ready to stimulate your abdominals with a more challenging workout, you are ready to go. But let's lay out some ground rules before you start strapping on the weight vest or grabbing the heaviest dumbbell you can.

RULES FOR SAFE RESISTANCE TRAINING

As I described earlier, the weight barrier does not have to weigh as much as your car for you to feel the results. By now you have learned to approach your abdominal region in a more functional way with reasonable goals for a stronger, tighter midsection.

- Start all the exercises without added resistance for 1 complete set, so you can learn the technique and engage the proper muscles first.
- Start with just enough resistance to make it hard for you to complete 2 entire sets.
- Maintain proper form, as well as muscle and spinal alignment, throughout the entire exercise routine.
- If you become fatigued early in your set, reduce the resistance or eliminate it completely before finishing your set.
- If you feel any pain in any region whatsoever, stop immediately and reevaluate your body mechanics while performing the movement. Do not do the exercise with resistance. If you continue to have pain, seek out medical help to rule out any underlying problems you may have.

Would it be easier just to use the abdominal machines in the gym? If you are still thinking this way, go back to the beginning of the book and reread Chapter 2 on the hip flexor muscles.

I don't like the machines you have to climb into, because all of us are different sizes and shapes. No matter which manufacturer made the exercise equipment, they can't fit us all properly, which results in improper use of our muscles, not only in the core region but also in the shoulders, arms, back, hips, and thighs. Also, many people are looking to work out without any special equipment beyond the bench or chair and a few weights or resistance bands to get rock-hard abs. The AbSmart system can easily be done anywhere. Let's get started.

Weighted Sit-Backs

Muscles emphasized: Upper and lower abdominals

1. Begin by sitting upright with your knees bent and your feet flat on the floor in front of you underneath a pair of dumbbells.

2. Holding light dumbbell weights in each of your hands, raise your arms straight in front of you to chest height.

3. Exhale as you contract your abdominals and lean back, keeping your hands in front of your body until you have reached the halfway point. Hold this position for 2 seconds.

4. Extend your arms out to the sides, and hold them at shoulder height for 2 seconds. Keeping a slight bend in your elbows, return to the start position and repeat the entire exercise.

Key Points to Remember

- Focus on contracting your abdominal muscles during the entire activity.

- Do not use momentum to get you through the exercise.

- Do not throw your arms out in front of you or to the sides. Rather, force yourself to focus on your core for strength.

- If you are too weak or fatigue too quickly at first, bend your arms while holding the weights or do not use weights during the exercise to start, and build up gradually.

- Do not do this exercise if you have lower-back issues.

7.1a, b
Weighted
Sit-Backs

Arm Circles with Dumbbell

Muscles emphasized: Upper and lower abdominals and obliques

1. Begin by lying on your back with your arms stretched up and holding a dumbbell above your head. Bend your knees, and place your feet flat on the floor.

2. Contract your abdominals before starting the arm movement.

3. Keeping your arms stretched in front of you, raise your shoulders and head off the floor. Move the weight in a clockwise circle all the way around until you return to the beginning point of the circle.

7.2a
Arm Circles with
Dumbbell

7.2b
Arm Circles with
Dumbbell

7.2c
Arm Circles with
Dumbbell

7.2d
Arm Circles with
Dumbbell

4. After completing your repetitions in a clockwise direction, without resting repeat counterclockwise until the set is complete.

5. Breathe deeply throughout the movement.

Key Points to Remember

- Focus on bringing your head and shoulders up far enough to feel the upper and lower abdominals engaged in the exercise.

- Concentrate on contracting your abdominal muscles during the entire activity.

- Do not pull with the arms; rather, use them as resistance and to guide you through the movement.

Side Ankle Touches with Dumbbell

Muscles emphasized: Obliques and upper abdominals

1. Begin by lying on your back with your legs straight; raise your legs so your toes are pointing toward the ceiling. Your arms should be outstretched above your head while holding onto a dumbbell.

2. Pull in your abdominals as you raise your hands toward your right ankle. Hold for 1 second, and then come halfway down.

3. Cross over toward your left ankle. Hold for 1 second, and return to the start position.

7.3a, b
Side Ankle
Touches with
Dumbbell

7.3c
Side Ankle Touches with
Dumbbell

Key Points to Remember

- Don't jerk yourself up during the movement.

- Focus on feeling all your muscle groups working.

- Concentrate on contracting all your lower abdominal muscles at the top of the motion.

- Don't hold your breath when performing this movement; that will only limit your range of motion.

- Do not turn this movement into an upper-arm exercise by emphasizing your arms swinging up.

- Do not lead with your head by lifting it faster than your arms.

Knee Push Isometrics

Muscles emphasized: Upper and lower abdominals

1. Lying on your back, bend your knees, and place your feet on the floor.

2. Pull your knees toward your chest, lifting your feet off the floor, until your knees are directly over your hips.

3. Place your hands on the front of your thighs, and push against them as you raise your upper body. Hold for 5 seconds, curl down your upper body and legs, and repeat.

7.4a
Knee Push Isometrics

7.4b
Knee Push Isometrics

Key Points to Remember

- Don't jerk yourself up; instead, press as hard as you can during the movement. Focus on feeling all your muscles groups working.

- Concentrate on contracting all your lower abdominal muscles at the top of the motion.

- Don't hold your breath when performing this movement; that will only limit your range of motion.

- Do not turn this movement into an upper-arm exercise by emphasizing your arms pressing against your legs.

- Contract your abdominals before you raise your upper body as far as possible.

What sets the next exercises apart from a typical crunch movement is that you try to raise yourself as high as you can without activating your stronger hip flexors, discussed in Chapter 2. Remember not to jerk yourself up into the positions. Instead, contract and use your abdominal muscles during the entire movements.

Walking-Up Leg Climb

Muscles emphasized: Upper and lower abdominals

1. Start by lying on your back as if you are going to perform a crunch, with your knees bent and feet flat on the floor. Place your hands by your sides with your low back flat.

2. Raise your left leg toward the ceiling with a slight bend in your knee.

3. While keeping your right foot flat on the floor, reach with your left hand around the back of your left leg at hamstring height as you lift your upper body.

7.5a
Walking-Up Leg Climb

7.5b
Walking-Up Leg Climb

7.5c, d
Walking-Up
Leg Climb

4. Reach with your right hand and place it behind your left calf as you continually pull in your abdominals and straighten your back.

5. Reach farther with your left hand, followed by your right hand, and hold onto your left ankle. Hold this position for 2 seconds. Slowly lower back down, moving hand over hand until your body has reached the floor again. Repeat on the opposite leg. Alternate back and forth throughout the set.

Long Leg Raise While Holding Support

Muscles emphasized: Upper and lower abdominals

1. Lie on your back with your legs fully extended and your head next to a sturdy object like the end of a workout bench, a bed, or a couch—anything that will be stable and secure and that you can firmly grip. Grasp this object above the top of your head. Pull in your abdominal muscles, and exhale as you lift your legs with a slight bend in the knees, curling up toward your face as you begin to raise your legs straight up toward the ceiling.

2. Continue to raise your hips off the floor as you further pull in your abdominal muscles and tighten your core, raising your body to a 90-degree angle with the floor while holding firmly with your hands. Your

7.6a
Long Leg Raise While
Holding Support

7.6b, c
Long Leg Raise While
Holding Support

weight should be on your upper back muscles, not your neck. If you feel pressure on your neck, you have gone too far over and must come back down until you no longer feel the pressure in your neck.

3. Inhale at the top of the movement, and move your legs slightly apart, about 3 to 4 inches, while contracting your glutes and core further.

4. Exhale while lowering your body with control and maintaining the straight line of your body, then curl your legs back down toward your chest. Keep your core and hands strongly engaged. Continue to lower your legs all the way back to the floor. Repeat the movement.

Key Points to Remember

- Focus on lowering yourself by using your core muscles, rather than just dropping down during the movement.

- Concentrate on contracting all your lower abdominal muscles during the entire exercise, not just at the beginning of the movement.

- Don't hold your breath when performing this movement; that will only limit your range of motion.

Medicine Ball Knee-Ups

Muscles emphasized: Lower and upper abdominals

1. Begin by sitting at the edge of a flat bench. Place a medicine ball between your knees. Squeeze and hold the medicine ball in place by gripping with your inner thigh muscles. (You can also use ankle weights in place of the medicine ball for this exercise.) Raise your feet off the ground. Lightly grip the edge of the bench to stabilize your body. Maintain a straight back throughout the movement; refrain from caving your spine inward.

2. Exhale and flex your hips, drawing your knees and thus the ball toward your midsection.

7.7a, b
Medicine Ball
Knee-Ups

3. Inhale and lower your knees back toward the ground without letting your feet touch the floor. Strive for fluidity of motion, rather than muscling up or using momentum to lift the legs upward.

Advanced Movement

Stretch your hands out to the sides when performing the exercise, rather than holding onto the bench.

Inner-Thigh Squeeze with Lift on Swiss Ball

Muscles emphasized: Lower abdominals, spinal erectors, glutes, inner and outer thighs

1. Start by lying on your back with your back flat and your arms by your sides. Place your legs on either side of a Swiss ball, holding the ball with your calf muscles against the side of the ball.

2. Squeezing your core muscles as you exhale, raise your hips off the floor while squeezing the ball with your legs throughout the movement. Hold for 2 seconds at the top. Lower your hips to the start position, just touching the floor with your glutes, and repeat.

Key Points to Remember

- Make sure you are pulling in your abdominals throughout the movement and not resting your midsection while holding onto the ball with your legs.

- Breathe in and out at regular intervals during the entire exercise.

7.8
Inner-Thigh Squeeze
with Lift on Swiss Ball

Side Push-Up Bridges with Dumbbells

Muscles emphasized: Lower abdominals, obliques, spinal erectors, and shoulders

This is a more advanced movement of the side push-up bridges. Before you progress to this exercise, make sure you can perform the side push-up position equally well on both sides of your body.

1. Begin in the push-up position with your hands resting on a pair of dumbbells on the floor set shoulder-width apart.

2. Raise your right arm holding the dumbbell straight up toward the ceiling while contracting your abdominal muscles, and hold yourself up in this position.

3. After completing your repetitions on one side, without resting repeat on the opposite side until the set is complete.

4. Breathe deeply throughout the movement.

Key Points to Remember

- Focus on turning with your midsection; this ensures complete activation of your oblique muscles.

- Try to hold yourself up without bending at your waist or relaxing your lower back muscles when performing this exercise.

- Concentrate on balancing with your core, rather than just your arm strength.

Exercise success is a matter of feeling the right muscles working at the right time. To get into that zone of combining your core muscle groups, you need to know and activate the right muscles, rather than just going through the motions and never fully activating the muscles you're trying to exercise. Keep your awareness on your body position and alignment of your neck, shoulders, lower back, hips, and abdominals throughout the exercise. This ensures that you get the best results from your training efforts.

7.9a
Side Push-Up Bridges with
Dumbbells

7.9b
Side Push-Up Bridges with
Dumbbells

Now let's move on to the next chapter, where you will learn to put a routine of combination exercises together so you can work out progressively for that firmer, stronger waistline.

CHAPTER SUMMARY

- Use the full range of motion.
- Control the speed of each movement and repetition.
- Experiment with the resistance, making adjustments by adding or removing weight as you become fatigued or are not feeling the proper muscles working during the exercise.
- Use gravity; do not just relax down to the start positions. Always be aware of your core stabilizing muscles, so they are not relaxed during the entire movement.
- Always choose quality of movement over quantity.

PART 3

Putting It All Together: The AbSmart Fitness Plan

CHAPTER 8

THE ULTIMATE CORE-CONDITIONING CIRCUIT

Proper strength and coordination are required to perform the more advanced exercises. Therefore, beginners should start with the basic movements for each exercise. As your strength and coordination increase, you can incorporate more advanced exercises into your routine. You should be more concerned about your form than reaching a certain number of repetitions. By focusing on your form first, you will be laying a foundation for proper body mechanics, good posture, and proper use of the appropriate muscles doing the action. If you fatigue early, take a short break before continuing, and maintain good form throughout your exercise program.

On the subject of repetitions, you'll hear one person or another give all sorts of reasons and arguments why you should do x amount to get results, and you'll hear an entirely different take from each on why you should do it his or her way. I am sure there will always be some authoritative source offering the latest "facts" about the right amount of repetitions or number of exercises we should perform to create a complete package for our efforts.

From the viewpoint of strength training, though, the following guidelines have been for years considered the classic understanding of how the muscle fiber fatigues and how strength is built on an anatomical and cellular level:

- 1 to 5 repetitions—power
- 5 to 10 repetitions—strength
- 10 to 12 repetitions—strength and definition to your muscles
- 12 to 15 repetitions—muscle definition
- 15 or more repetitions—muscular endurance

The most important factor, however, is how many repetitions it takes you to feel your muscles contract and how long your muscles take to fatigue before you need a rest.

I have trained with top-level athletes in their sports as well as the most out-of-condition person recovering from surgery. What I have seen is that some individuals can contract their abdominal muscles more easily, finding that perfect zone with fewer repetitions, while for others it takes much more to stimulate their muscle groups. While most will be able to perform the movements for longer time periods as they become more efficient at the exercise, that progress may not be a sign of becoming stronger in a true sense.

Use repetitions as a general guideline, not a set rule you must follow. Focus on fully working your muscles at a good pace. Keep your rest periods to the minimum—that is, just enough time to recover and start again.

Determine your goals. Choose exercises based on your training experience (beginner, intermediate, advanced) and whether you want to build (more difficult exercises for lower reps) or streamline (easier exercises for higher repetitions for your midsection).

KEY COMPONENTS THAT SHOULD GUIDE YOU THROUGH YOUR WORKOUTS

Before starting your workout, review what you want to accomplish in your workout. Keep the following components in mind.

- **Pick the best time to train your abdominals.** You've probably heard it before, but a great time to exercise is in the morning because the rest of the day doesn't get in the way. It sets the right tone for the day, and you don't have to find time or energy later on. If the morning doesn't suit you, then anchor your workout slot to some other daily routine. Just don't try to work your midsection right after eating.

- **Target particular areas of your midsection,** including the upper abs, lower abs, and obliques (sides). Choose movements that work individual areas as well as combination exercises. Start with the most difficult exercises first, when your abs are strongest. Typically, lower abs are weakest in most people and require the most coordinated movement patterns, so I would recommend this as a good area in which to start.

- **Hit all areas of your midsection.** Use different exercises to ensure that you've got all the areas covered, or do complete workouts that target just one area, and then hit the others in the following workouts.
  - **Upper and lower abdominals.** Though the rectus abdominis is one muscle, you can work the lower region more effectively by securing your upper body and flexing your hips and pelvis toward your rib cage. Keeping your lower body stable and curling your upper torso toward your hips works the upper section of your waistline in general. For practical purposes, you can't totally isolate one region from another, but you can emphasize one region or the other. Remember what area of your midsection you are trying to focus on with the exercise, and concentrate on that region.
  - **Obliques.** The obliques are called upon for all rotating and twisting motions of your waistline. Most upper- and lower-abdominal exercises can be modified to incorporate the obliques by directing your shoulder toward the opposite knee or by angling a knee toward the opposite shoulder. Many of the core functional movements in this book allow you to engage the front, back, and sides of your waistline all at once.

- **Vary your exercise order.** Experimenting with the order of exercises will keep your workout fresh and invigorating. Add variations and new exercises to keep your abs from adapting to a particular routine. How often should you make a switch? It depends. Are you still sore after your workouts? Then your body hasn't adapted yet to the workout. Once you lose that soreness after a workout or can perform all the exercises too easily, it's time to change your workout.

- **Focus on proper spinal alignment.** Although your spine flexes during many ab movements, keep your cervical spine (neck region), head, and shoulders in alignment while exercising; don't press your chin into your chest. Don't interlock your hands behind your head and pull on it, which can disrupt your alignment. Instead, cup your hands behind your ears to gently support your head.

- **Stay in control.** As with any exercise, your midsection exercises should be performed with strict form in a controlled manner. This will minimize the risk of injury. Focusing on your movements increases the intensity of the exercise with forceful contractions rather than momentum. Prevent yourself from swinging and straining through a movement, as that may lead to an injury.

- **Go slow.** Do your abdominal exercises with strict form in a slow, controlled manner to minimize the risk of injury. Smooth movements increase the intensity of contraction and reduce momentum.

- **Feel the contraction.** Focus on feeling the contraction of your abdominal region while exercising, and really squeeze your muscles. You may find it helpful to place one hand on your midsection at first to see if you are really contracting your muscles. At the top of the range of motion, momentarily hesitate or hold the contraction forcefully, squeezing your midsection.

- **Maintain muscle tension.** Don't rest between repetitions. To maintain constant tension on your waistline, stop just short of the endpoint during the relaxation phase of your movement. If you have back problems, relax completely between sets to rest your lumbar muscles; they fatigue faster than your midsection will.

- **Use the entire range of motion.** Exercising your abdominal region can effectively be done through a complete range of motion, as with all the other exercises you use for other parts of your body. Don't use short choppy movements to train your abs.

- **Breathe!** When exercising your midsection, breathe in through your nose during the relaxation phase, and exhale during contraction. While this is a general suggestion, you may feel that you need to breathe more often near the end of your exercise routine to maintain your strength and rhythm. Just remember not to hold your breath, and you'll do fine.

- **Keep the beat.** Like a composer or musician playing an instrument, find that natural groove and pace in exercising your midsection. Adjust your timing and your breathing, especially near the end of your workout, to keep your rhythm smooth.

- **Choose your resistance.** The weight used in abdominal training typically consists of nothing more than your own body weight. If your abdominals are weak or you're just starting a new program, consider easier variations without added resistance. As you progress, you can change arm and foot positions to increase the difficulty, placing more tension in the region you are exercising. You can further increase the difficulty by adding light weights or changing the angle of an exercise. Regardless, the appropriate resistance should be used to allow you to complete the desired number of repetitions.

- **Adjust your rest periods.** After completing your full set, rest long enough to recover from that set before starting the next set. At first you may take longer rest periods until you are used to the exercise. As you advance and become stronger, you'll cut back on the amount of resting. As a general rule, 30 seconds to 1 minute should be enough time to catch your breath and proceed with your workout.

- **Add variety.** Once you master the basic abdominal and core exercises, add different movements to help prevent the muscles from becoming accustomed to the same exercises and to allow them to be stressed from different angles, maximizing your routine by ensuring greater muscle involvement. This will help prevent boredom with your workouts and training plateaus.

- **Adjust intensity for your goals.** How difficult is it for you to do the movement? How much can you do, and for how long? For example, decreasing the number of seconds that you rest between your exercises and/or sets of movements will affect your overall condition and how your midsection will respond to your workouts. By shortening your rest periods, you will build up your muscular and aerobic endurance.

- **Adjust the volume.** Volume is the combination of the total number of sets and repetitions of your exercises. You should not increase both intensity and the number of sets (volume) you perform in the same workout, for this will lead to burnout and injuries. Rather, raise the number of sets or repetitions for one or two particular movements before adding a harder exercise or more exercises in the same workout period.

- **Recover between workouts.** As with exercising any other muscle group, give yourself plenty of time to recover from your previous workout so you are well rested and ready to push yourself to another level in your workouts.

- **Work your lower back muscles.** To support and stabilize your spinal region, don't neglect to train your lower back muscles. Your core consists of at least four sides—lower and upper front, sides, back, and of course the deeper muscle groups in the pelvis wall and spine. Make sure you exercise them all.

ASPECTS OF FATIGUE AND STRENGTH

In a program of this nature, both short-term and long-term fatigue must be recognized. In terms of proper recovery, it's important to always address the immediate aspects of fatigue (felt in your muscles immediately after the exercise), rather than the accumulating aspects of fatigue as your training continues. Specific ranges of motion are important to fatigue as you target a particular region in your core training from one workout to the next.

To properly strengthen a weaker area in your core—say, your lower abdominal region—you should emphasize exercising these muscles first in your routine with specific chosen movements. This will allow you to increase that region's capacity for exercise tolerance, with the result being a stronger all-around core region.

When you combine traditional and nontraditional movements and the science behind strength, conditioning, and functional training, you will produce a workout that will transform your core region beyond your expectations. By using the sequence circuit training, combining functional exercises and traditional training methods, you will produce a routine that will transform your midsection, glutes, and lower back muscles, all in one workout.

You can adjust your intensity level anytime by slowing down the pace, and you can change the rhythm of the entire routine by using planks for rest periods. In these ways, you can add the benefit of cardio training as well, burning more calories in your workouts.

The AbSmart system offers multiple benefits for any hard-training athlete or person who is serious about getting his or her midsection into shape. Not only does this type of training increase your overall conditioning, it also translates into better results for other exercises and for exercising other regions of your body. Additionally, this program will save you valuable training time without wasted movements done with improper techniques. Keep these key components in mind as you put your routine together in the next section.

CORE-CONDITIONING CIRCUIT TRAINING

When you first start working your core, it's easier to stimulate your muscles and feel your muscles responding to the exercises. As you increase your strength and endurance and move on to more advanced movements, you will need to change your workouts frequently in order to consistently challenge yourself and avoid a workout rut.

Now that you have learned the abdominal movements, it's time to put them into an order or sequence—a pattern of exercises performed right after each other to keep your workouts challenging and productive. Don't worry if you cannot complete the entire set of recommended exercises at first. Over a short period of time, you will develop stronger, firmer abdominal muscles, and you'll be flying through the routine in no time at all.

The repetitions that are recommended are a guideline. What I've learned from many years of training with professional athletes and people recovering from back surgery is that each individual gets a muscle pump (muscle fullness) at different times during the exercise and will fatigue the muscle group faster or slower, depending on the rate of movement and muscle fatigue. In other words, your body will let you know when you have had enough. When you cannot perform the exercise smoothly or feel your muscles working correctly, it's time for a break.

A general rule is that the more fit you are at the beginning of this program and the more muscle endurance you have, the more repetitions per exercise you'll be able to complete before muscle fatigue sets in. The key point for beginners to remember is that you should not stop doing the exercise because you are unable to complete all the recommended repetitions for just one exercise. Move on to the next movement. Over time, you'll develop enough strength and muscle endurance to complete all of your repetitions and sets, and you'll be able to feel—and see—the difference.

SUGGESTED NUMBERS OF SETS AND REPETITIONS

Throughout the book, I have suggested how the AbSmart system is a holistic approach to exercising rather than a regimen to follow. Use these suggestions to that effect—you may be able to do one movement more while another less. The key is consistency.

- Beginners should start with 12 to 15 repetitions and complete an entire sequence 3 times before adding repetitions to your routine.
- At the intermediate level, start with 15 to 20 repetitions as you complete 4 sets of sequences, and then move up to the advanced level.
- Advanced exercisers should start with 20 to 30 repetitions for 3 sequences before adding more repetitions or exercises to your routine.

For Advanced Exercisers

If you are an abdominal expert, you already know your body's adaptability and should be feeling the movements more than when you first started to work out. The advanced person needs to look out for routine in your workout. It's all too easy to become so comfortable with your training that you just knock out the repetitions without focusing on the movement. Stay sharp and change your exercises around constantly for further results.

TIPS FOR INDIVIDUALIZING YOUR WORKOUT

- Determine your goals based on whether you want to build (do more difficult exercises for lower reps) or streamline (do easier exercises for higher repetitions for your midsection).
- Choose exercises based on your training experience—beginner, intermediate, or advanced.
- Use repetitions as a general guideline, not a set rule you must follow.
- Focus on fully working your muscles at a good pace. Keep your rest periods to the minimum—just enough to recover and start again.

SUGGESTED SEQUENCES

Start these sequences at the top of the list and on alternate workout days; after a while, when the routine gets easy switch to starting from the bottom of the list and move up. Don't be afraid to change the order of the movements. If you feel your muscles working better with a different order, so be it. And before you start your abdominal routine, remember to stretch out your hip flexors, as demonstrated in Chapter 3.

Beginner Workout 1

For each exercise, do 3 sets of 12 to 20 repetitions.

Psoas stretch without chair

Psoas stretch while facing chair

Can opener

Alternating double
ankle touches

Two-inch crunch

Crisscross leg pull-ins

Beginner Workout 2

For each exercise, do 3 sets of 12 to 20 repetitions.

Psoas bench stretch

Side arm squeezes

Cross-over crunches

Double-knee pull-ins

Beginner Workout 3

For each exercise, do 3 sets of 12 to 20 repetitions.

Psoas stretch while
facing chair

Crisscross leg pull-ins

Arm circles

Side elbow bridges

When doing intermediate and advanced workouts, do your stretches before and after your abdominal workouts. Your goal is to complete the sequence all the way through without stopping before moving on to the next sequence with 3 to 4 sets of 12 to 25 repetitions per movement.

Intermediate Sequence 1

Elevated butterflies   Two-inch crunch

Cross-over crunches   Advanced
                                       froggies

Advanced can opener
with leg raised

Intermediate Sequence 2

Double-knee pull-ins

Seated bicycle rotations

Hip turns with crunch

Alternating double
ankle touches

Advanced
froggies

Intermediate Sequence 3

Two-inch crunch

Hip turns with crunch

Seated bicycle rotations

Seated froggy with
arm rotation

Arm circles

Advanced
froggies

Swiss ball turns

Seated torsal rotation

Hip turns with crunch

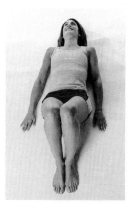

Pocket reaches

Intermediate Sequence 5

Advanced can opener
with leg raised

Side bridges with knee raises

Straight-leg bicycles

Elevated butterflies

Elevated corkscrews

Alternating double
ankle touches

Advanced Sequence 1

Seated torsal rotation

Plank jacks

Pocket reaches

Side elbow bridges

Side arm squeezes

Super abs

Advanced Sequence 2

Two-inch crunch

Side arm squeezes

Side-turning ankle touches

Straight-leg bicycles

Hip turns with crunch

Advanced
froggies

Advanced Sequence 3

Advanced can opener
with leg raised

Sideways elbow-to-leg touches

Elevated corkscrews

Super abs

Worm planks

Seated froggy with
arm rotation

Pocket reaches

Knee push isometrics

Advanced Sequence 4

Alternating double   Elevated corkscrews
ankle touches

Side-turning ankle touches

Hip turns with crunch

Side arm squeezes

Elevated butterflies

Plank wide leg raises

➤

Advanced Sequence 4 *(continued)*

Side push-up bridges

Walking-up leg climb

Super abs

Advanced Sequence 5

Two-inch crunch

Alternating double
ankle touches

Hip turns with crunch

Medicine ball knee-ups

➤

Advanced Sequence 5 *(continued)*

Inner-thigh squeeze with lift on Swiss ball

Straight-leg bicycles

Two-inch crunch

Advanced can opener
with leg raised

Elevated butterflies

Side arm squeezes

Side ankle touches with dumbbell

Side push-up bridges with dumbbells

SEVEN-MINUTE WORKOUTS

For when you are on the run, I have created a few seven-minute workouts that you can do first thing in the morning or on your lunch break if you cannot get your regular workout in. This routine is fast but very effective for getting the results you want. Do 15 to 20 repetitions of each exercise for a total of 2 sets in less than 10 minutes.

Seven-Minute Sequence 1

Hip turns with crunch

Worm planks

Side-turning ankle touches

Cross-over crunches

Alternating double
ankle touches

Pocket reaches

Knee push isometrics

Straight-leg bicycles

Seven-Minute Sequence 3

Alternating double
ankle touches

Straight-leg bicycles

Elevated corkscrews

Knee push isometrics

You are halfway there. In the next chapters, we are going to focus on why your stomach responds the way it does to foods and how to improve on shrinking your waistline by applying some simple guidelines for eating.

CHAPTER SUMMARY

- **Target for efficiency.** When you look at your midsection in the mirror, what do you see that could use more of your efforts? Your lower abs or the sides? Focus on one or two areas that you want to improve upon, and do the exercises that target that area. Make sure to work out that area first, when you are at your strongest.

- **Preparation pays off in many ways.** Laying out your workout, knowing what you want to accomplish rather that just winging it, will make your effort much more effective. Always stretch out your hip flexors before starting your abdominal routine. The time used for stretching before training your abs will pay you back in dividends, workout after workout, with a stronger and slimmer core.

- **Use inspiration, not just perspiration.** Time and time again, I see people swinging their bodies back and forth or jerking their heads up and down while training, with very little results. It would be better to see how you can turn and move into different positions to stimulate your muscle groups without repeating the same exercises over and over again.

- **Results are what matter.** Don't follow other people's recommendations on how to perform a certain exercise if you can't feel your muscles working. Stop and evaluate your efforts, and change the angle slightly or hold the positions a little bit longer. Or change around the order in which you perform the movement to get the results you are after.

- **Don't get too comfortable!** As you become more comfortable with the sequences, you can change them up and exercise with more intensity while enhancing your skills and endurance in your core region. An important part of your routine is to use more calories than you eat in order to stimulate your metabolism. The only way to achieve this is through a combination of diet and regular exercise. For maximum fat loss, you should try for cardio training for 60 minutes, preferably five to seven days per week. The National Academy of Sciences recommends that people who want to lose weight should exercise moderately at least 60 minutes a day. Sure, that sounds like a lot, but as more studies come out, we are finding that you can break up that amount of time and see and feel the results.

CHAPTER 9

WHAT TO EAT FOR A LEAN AND HEALTHY WAISTLINE

Rather than simply saying, "Here, eat these magical foods, and your waistline will shrink," I would like to discuss the mechanics of eating. Don't worry, I do offer alternative food choices for you to select over higher-fat or sugar-coated foods. But what is a diet plan really? Eating reasonably comes to mind—enjoying foods that are not only nutritious and healthful but also tasty. Why suffer through eating plain foods, half starving, getting angrier by the end of the week, and then blowing it over the weekend by stuffing yourself with toxic foods? Is it really worth your effort and eventual guilt?

Often we hear we must eat certain specific foods to shrink our waist and lose weight, only to end up spinning our wheels just trying to figure out how to eat to maximize fat loss. In this chapter, I try to tackle these issues and untangle the misinformation that might be holding you back from shaping up your midsection and dropping a few pounds in the process.

If you want to live a longer, healthier life, start off slowly. Gradually, you'll build up a tolerance for new kinds of foods and not even notice how healthful they are. Treat yourself to new cuisine once a month until you are eating a variety of foods all the time. Forget about giving up junk food cold turkey—it will just drive you mad and those around you madder. Following are some nutritional food sources to incorporate into your daily diet to help prevent bloating and weight retention.

FIBER

Eat more fiber. You've probably heard it before. Dietary fiber is found mainly in fruits, vegetables, whole grains, and legumes. But do you know why fiber is so good for your health? Fiber is probably best known for its ability to prevent or relieve constipation, so there will be less bloating of your midsection. But fiber also can provide other health benefits, such as lowering your risk of diabetes and heart disease by moving and binding foods as the fiber goes through your digestive tract. By binding with other foods, fiber helps reduce spikes in your glucose levels after a meal.

Increasing the amount of fiber you eat each day isn't difficult. Find out how much you eat now by looking at the labels on food products, and learn to include more high-fiber foods in your meals and snacks. This will help you feel full because high-fiber foods generally require more chewing time, which gives your body time to register when you're no longer hungry. This way, you're less likely to overeat, so fiber may also help with weight loss. A fiber-rich diet tends to make a meal feel larger and linger longer, so you stay full for a longer time. Also, fiber tends to be less "energy dense," which means there are fewer calories for the same volume of food.

Which Type of Fiber Is Best?

Dietary fiber includes parts of plant foods that your body can't digest or absorb. It is often classified into two categories:

- **Insoluble fiber.** This type of fiber doesn't dissolve in water. It increases the movement of food material through your digestive system and increases stool bulk, so it can benefit those who have irregular bowel movements or struggle with constipation. Sources include whole wheat flour, wheat bran, vegetables, and nuts.

- **Soluble fiber.** This type of fiber does dissolve in water. It can help lower blood cholesterol and glucose levels. Soluble-fiber foods generally require more chewing time, which gives your body time to register when you're no longer hungry, so you're less likely to overeat. Also, a high-fiber diet tends to make a meal feel larger and linger longer, so you stay full longer. Sources include apples, citrus fruits, oats, peas, beans, barley, and psyllium.

The amount of each type of fiber varies in different foods. How much fiber do you need each day? The National Academy of Sciences Institute of Medicine, which provides science-based advice on matters of medicine and health, gives the following daily recommendations for adults:

	Age 50 and Younger	Age 51 and Older
Men	38 g	30 g
Women	25 g	21 g

Tips for Getting Your Fiber

As you will see from this list, it's not that hard to get your fill of fiber-rich foods without going out of your way to do so.

- Start your day with a high-fiber breakfast cereal containing 5 or more grams of fiber per serving. If you add soy milk instead of cow's milk, it will contribute 6 more grams of fiber to your meal.
- Add oats or bran cereal to baked goods such as homemade cookies, breads, salads, and sauces. You'll be delighted and will hardly notice the added fiber if you add small amounts at a time to these food sources.
- Buy whole-grain breads.
- Substitute whole-grain flour for white flour when baking bread. Start with a quarter cup and gradually build up to completely replacing the white flour.
- New to the market is white whole wheat flour. Try it if you can't seem to get around the color differences between whole wheat and white flour.
- Eat whole wheat pasta.
- Eat more beans and lentils. Add beans to soups or salads. Snack on edamame (soybeans harvested while green), which has 7 grams of fiber per serving.
- Snack on fresh and dried fruit and raw vegetables.

I like to drink a fiber supplement after meals sometimes, and I snack on organic fiber bars that contain 14 grams of fiber per serving. As you can see, there are many ways to add fiber to your diet. When you do, it will help you digest your foods better and slim your waist.

CARBOHYDRATES AND SANDWICHES

Everyone's body reacts differently to carbs. If carbs such as white breads, white bagels, and white tortillas make you gain weight and feel bloated, you know that you should avoid them to some degree. To limit carb intake or get healthier carbs into your diet, try asking for whole wheat bread or buns, use a whole wheat pita with your hummus, and so on. If there are no options but white bread, eat half of your sandwich with the bread and the other half without. If you do that, you should have enough protein to balance out the rest of your meal to maintain your sugar levels without spiking them too high by consuming the entire white bun.

Whole Grains

Whole grains retain the bran and germ as well as the endosperm, as opposed to refined grains, which retain only the endosperm. The bran is the coarse outer layer of the grain. It contains about 50 to 80 percent of the minerals in grains, as well as fiber and other bioactive components. The endosperm is the middle layer, accounting for about 85 percent of a whole grain by weight. It contains mostly carbohydrates, along with small amounts of B vitamins. The germ is the smallest of the three components.

The following whole-grain products are commonly known and nutritious:

- Oatmeal: Thanks to whole grains, this cereal takes longer than most commercial cold cereal to digest, resulting in a slower energy release and a longer-lasting feeling of being full.
- Brown rice: Compared with white rice, brown rice has a higher fiber content and is more nutritionally dense.
- Whole wheat flour and whole wheat bread: These whole-grain alternatives give you more nutrition than refined flour and breads and take longer to digest, resulting in a fuller feeling, so you eat less.

In contrast, the following products are made with refined grains:

- White bread
- White rice
- Many store-bought pastas (However, there are whole-grain varieties of pasta available in most food sections of stores, with other pasta varieties.)

Identifying Whole-Grain Products. You can identify whole-grain products by reading the ingredient list. Typically, if the ingredient list says "whole wheat" or "whole meal" in the name of the first ingredient, the product is a whole-grain food item. Another way to identify whole grains in the foods you eat is to look at the nutritional facts on the label to see whether the food item contains dietary fiber. If it contains a significant amount, it most likely contains whole grains. "Wheat flour" generally is not a whole grain and therefore does not indicate a whole-grain product.

Many types of bread are colored brown (often with molasses) and made to look like whole grain, even though they are not. Additionally, some food manufacturers make foods with a small amount of whole-grain ingredients. If whole-grain ingredients are not the dominant ingredient (listed first), they are not whole-grain products.

Whole-grain products have a label listing both whole wheat and whole grain, or 100 percent whole wheat. Whole grains are typically more expensive than refined grains because their higher oil content makes them susceptible to becoming rancid, which complicates processing, storage, and transport.

Health Benefits. Whole grains are nutritionally better than refined grains, richer in dietary fiber, antioxidants, and protein. They also contain important minerals such as magnesium, manganese, phosphorus, and selenium, as well as vitamins B_6, E, and niacin.

The greater amount of dietary fiber—as much as four times higher than that found in refined grains—is likely the most important benefit. It has been shown to reduce the incidence of some forms of gastrointestinal diseases. Some of these protective effects occur because carbohydrates from whole grains are digested and enter the bloodstream more slowly.

WHOLE-GRAIN AND REFINED GRAIN PRODUCTS

Whole Wheat Bread (1 slice)	White Bread (1 slice)
Calories 70	Calories 67
Carbohydrate 13 g	Carbohydrate 12 g
Protein 3 g	Protein 2 g
Total fat 1.0 g	Total fat 0.9 g
Saturated fat 0.4 g	Saturated fat 0.1 g
Fiber 3.0 g	Fiber 0.57 g

continued

Croissant	Multi-Grain English Muffin
Calories 114	Calories 100
Carbohydrate 13 g	Carbohydrate 24 g
Protein 2 g	Protein 5 g
Total fat 8 g	Total fat 1 g
Saturated fat 3 g	Saturated fat 0 g
Fiber 1 g	Fiber 8 g

Bagel (100 grams)	Pita Bread (100 grams)
Calories 272	Calories 278
Carbohydrate 53 g	Carbohydrate 55 g
Protein 11 g	Protein 9 g
Total fat 2 g	Total fat 1 g
Saturated fat 0 g	Saturated fat 0 g
Fiber 0 g	Fiber 1 g

NEED PROTEIN? GO FISH!

Protein helps curb your appetite, which can help you lose weight. Compared with carbs and fats—which are primarily energy sources—proteins also play crucial roles in the body. Protein provides structural features to your body and improves your immune system. Proteins in the form of enzymes and hormones help regulate sleep and digestion. When you get your protein from fish, you have the extra benefit of consuming omega-3 fatty acids, which help lower your cholesterol and decrease inflammation, resulting in less swelling in your GI tract.

By incorporating fish into your diet, you provide your body with nutrients and change your tastes for different foods. Also, in the process, you give your metabolism a break from digesting meats, which will help reduce bloating as well. You may want to try eating fish during the week, so you can get the freshest of fish, or ask the person behind your fish counter what the delivery days are for the fish of your choice. You can also use canned tuna or salmon for your protein source if fresh fish is not available. Start your morning with a lox and whole wheat bagel, or try it for lunch if you prefer. For dinner enjoy a fish taco or salmon fillet. Not only are these low in saturated fat, but they are also healthful sources of protein and omega-3 fatty acids for your cardiovascular system.

HEALTHY FISH CHOICES

**Fresh Atlantic Salmon
(6.3 oz.)**

Calories 367
Carbohydrate 0 g
Protein 39 g
Total fat 22 g
Saturated fat 4.5 g
Fiber 0 g

**Fresh Tilapia
(6.3 oz.)**

Calories 192
Carbohydrate 0 g
Protein 9 g
Total fat 3.4 g
Saturated fat 1 g
Fiber 0 g

Fresh Mahimahi (6.3 oz.)

Calories 173
Carbohydrate 0 g
Protein 37 g
Total fat 1.4 g
Saturated fat 0.5 g
Fiber 0 g

Fresh Tuna, Yellowfin (6.3 oz.)

Calories 184
Carbohydrate 0 g
Protein 39 g
Total fat 1.6 g
Saturated fat 0.4 g
Fiber 0 g

Fresh Pacific Cod (6.3 oz.)

Calories 190
Carbohydrate 0 g
Protein 39 g
Total fat 1.7 g
Saturated fat 0.4 g
Fiber 0 g

Fresh Halibut (6.3 oz.)

Calories 223
Carbohydrate 0 g
Protein 42 g
Total fat 4.7 g
Saturated fat 0.7 g
Fiber 0 g

**Salmon, Smoked Lox
(6.3 oz.)**

Calories 200
Carbohydrate 0 g
Protein 30 g
Total fat 7.4 g
Saturated fat 1.6 g
Fiber 0 g

**Canned White Tuna in Water
(6.3 oz.)**

Calories 220
Carbohydrate 0 g
Protein 40 g
Total fat 5.1 g
Saturated fat 1.4 g
Fiber 0 g

Warning: Lox is high in sodium at 2,400 milligrams, your maximum allowance for the day.

VEGETARIAN FOR THE DAY?

Another healthful approach to eating is to try a vegetarian diet. Wow, now I lost you, didn't I? You might be thinking I have gone too far by suggesting you eliminate all your important sources of protein to maintain and build muscles. Well, what happened to wanting to shrink your stomach down to size? Are you worried you'll become too thin to see? All the stereotypes people have of those who refrain from eating meats are not only exaggerated but also false.

In an Oxford Vegetarian Study, BMI (body mass index—a measure of body fat based on height and weight) values were higher in nonvegetarians than for vegetarians in all age groups, and for both men and women. In a study of men and women reported in the *British Medical Journal*, researchers compared the relationship between meat consumption and obesity among meat eaters, fish eaters, and vegetarians. In that study, the mean BMI was highest in the meat eaters and lowest in the vegans (those who eat no animal products at all). Factors that may help explain the lower BMI among vegetarians include differences in macronutrient content, such as lower fat and higher fiber consumption, as well as greater consumption of vegetables, which result in less body fat being stored on your body.

Open your eyes to the wonders of a vegan lifestyle, even if just for a day, and you'll feel the difference. You'll be lighter, less irritable, and actually taste the sweetness and textures of the foods you put into your mouth.

Beyond the Salad Bar

Not buying it yet? Why not try it for one meal a day for a week? You choose lunch or dinner. Then try an entire day without meat for all your meals. Have some fun with it. You don't have to just order salads. Why not try a vegetable stew or a veggie burrito?

Besides boiling or steaming, grilling vegetables that are in season will add fiber to your diet and variety at the same time. Go ahead and experiment with different sizes and types.

Dress Up Your Veggies

You don't have to boil your veggies every time. Instead enjoy them by cooking them on the grill.

- **Zucchini.** This vegetable works great on the grill. Cut lengthwise ⅓- to ½-inch-thick pieces about 3 to 4 inches long, about half a pound's worth. Pour olive oil over the vegetables, coating them evenly; you can also sprinkle some black pepper and garlic over them. Place them on the grill for about 5 to 8 minutes, depending on how hot your grill heat is. It doesn't take long and adds a delicious side dish to your meals that is fast and simple.

- **Bell pepper.** Remove the stem and seeds, and cut each pepper into quarters. Mix with olive oil and black pepper, and grill for about 5 to 10 minutes until the skin is blackened or charred. Goes great with sandwiches and with your eggs for breakfast.

- **Eggplant.** Cut into ⅓- to ½-inch-thick pieces crosswise, and mix with olive oil, garlic, and black pepper. Grill for 5 to 8 minutes until they are blackened or charred slightly, just until tender.

These three vegetables are most readily available in stores. For more ideas, check out other recipes in cookbooks or magazines. Also, if you Google one or two ingredients, you generally can get links to good recipes.

HEALTHY FROZEN FOOD CHOICES

Some of my favorite brands of ready-made vegan foods are listed here, compared with meat alternatives.

Morningstar Farms Veggie Corn Dogs	vs.	Hot Dog
Calories 150		Calories 210
Carbohydrate 22 g		Carbohydrate 0 g
Protein 7 g		Protein 6 g
Total fat 4 g		Total fat 10 g
Saturated fat 0.5 g		Saturated fat 3 g
Fiber 3 g		Fiber 2 g

continued

**Boca Meatless Burger,
All-American Flame Grilled   vs.   Beef Burger**

Calories 90	Calories 190
Carbohydrate 4 g	Carbohydrate 0 g
Protein 7 g	Protein 40 g
Total fat 3 g	Total fat 13 g
Saturated fat 1 g	Saturated fat 5 g
Fiber 3 g	Fiber 0 g

**Boca Meatless
Breakfast Links   vs.   Pork Sausage Links**

Calories 70	Calories 160
Carbohydrate 4 g	Carbohydrate 0 g
Protein 7 g	Protein 40 g
Total fat 3 g	Total fat 14 g
Saturated fat 0.5 g	Saturated fat 4 g
Fiber 20 g	Fiber 0 g

Boca Meatless Breakfast Wraps, Sausage, Egg, and Cheese

Calories 220
Carbohydrate 27 g
Protein 16 g
Total fat 7 g
Saturated fat 2.5 g
Fiber 6 g

These are just a few soy-based foods. Many other nutritional vegetarian food products are available in the frozen-food section of a good supermarket. Be sure that the sodium content is not too high; try to keep it below 400 grams per serving—less would be better.

WHAT'S FOR BREAKFAST?

The benefits of eating breakfast include a revved-up metabolism first thing in the morning, so your body burns the maximum number of calories to fuel your activities throughout the day. Also, people who eat a balanced breakfast consume fewer total calories throughout the day. Studies have shown that eating breakfast can be important for maintaining a healthy body weight.

Many people have a hard time making smart breakfast choices. Can't give up that sugary cold cereal or high-fat pastry in the morning? Or can't bear the thought of eating something boring like plain oatmeal without milk or sugar? If placing fruit on top of your hot porridge isn't your thing, no problem. Why not place a few ounces of your old sugary cereal on top of the more healthful cereal for a month or two? Day by day, gradually lessen the number of ounces you put on until you reach a manageable level where you can still taste the sweetness and learn to enjoy the healthful cereal. What does the trick for me is to add less than a palmful of my kids' sugary cereal on top of my high-fiber cereal. Isn't this more realistic than mustering up the courage to start your day by sitting down to another breakfast of sawdust and pebbles?

Eggs

While there are arguments for and against consumption of eggs, I think they are a rather good source of protein. Eggs have been given a bad rap because of their high cholesterol content, but they are low in saturated fat, and the jury is still out on whether there is a direct link between dietary cholesterol, which is found in the foods we eat, and blood cholesterol, which is manufactured by the body. So eggs enjoyed in moderation are a fine protein source.

To gradually make more healthful choices, the next time you make an omelet, start off with one and a half yolks with some egg whites. Then gradually move toward one yolk and two egg whites. Add veggies, such as mushrooms, tomatoes, onions, and green peppers, and some cheese to your omelet. With all those extras, you will no longer be missing that extra yolk.

Meat with Your Breakfast?

If you consume a protein source without any simple carbohydrates for breakfast, you will give your metabolism a steady form of energy, rather than a quick jolt from a breakfast cereal.

Add a little breakfast sausage to your meal in the morning. I like turkey sausages, as they are low in fat and lower in saturated fat than pork sausages. If you can't find those, look for beef sausages. With beef sausages, make sure there are no added chemicals to make it taste like something it really isn't. Food additives and preservatives can cause a bloating reaction (see Chapter 10). Another good alternative is soy-based sausages.

To start eating more soy, try half and half. Place one link of soy sausage next to your meat sausage, and eat them together. Not only will you be able to taste your meat choice, you'll fill up on a more healthful, fiber-rich food source, and soon you'll be eating just the soy. If not, that's fine; just eat both and trick your taste buds at the same time. Remember, there is a learning curve in everything that you try, including eating new foods.

HEALTHY FROZEN BREAKFAST CHOICES

Jimmy Dean Turkey Sausage Patties

Serving size: 2 patties (68 g)
Amount per serving:
Calories 120
Calories from fat 70
Total fat 7 g
Saturated fat 2 g
Trans fat 0 g
Cholesterol 55 mg
Sodium 490 mg
Total carbohydrate 1 g
Dietary fiber 0 g
Sugars 1 g
Protein 13 g

Morningstar Farms Veggie Breakfast, Sausage Patties

Total fat 3 g
Saturated fat 0.5 g
Polyunsaturated fat 2.0 g
Monounsaturated fat 0.5 g

Sodium 260 mg

Total carbohydrate 3 g

Dietary fiber 1 g

Sugars 1 g

Protein 10 g

Applegate Farms Chicken and Maple Sausage

Total fat 8 g

Saturated fat 2 g

Cholesterol 65 mg

Sodium 510 mg

Total carbohydrate 4 g

Sugars 4 g

Protein 14 g

GLYCEMIC INDEX: WHAT'S IT ALL ABOUT?

Finally, I would like to address the glycemic index. You have most likely heard of it by now. So what is this glycemic index all about, and is it worth considering as a way to help you control body weight? The glycemic index measures a food's impact on your blood glucose levels and the way your body tries to balance out an overload from your food by producing more insulin and using the glucose for muscle activity. Researchers have spent years debating what makes blood glucose levels too high. Potential culprits have included sugar, carbohydrates in general, simple carbs, starches, and more.

Why Is It Important?

Scientists have learned that foods with a high glycemic index generally make blood glucose levels higher. In addition, people who eat a lot of high-glycemic-index foods tend to have more body fat, as measured by the body mass index (BMI), which is linked to obesity, heart disease, and diabetes.

High-glycemic-index foods are ones that include many carbohydrates, such as cereal, pasta, rice, baked goods, and of course bread. As we have learned through research studies, low-glycemic-index foods are more healthful choices, because they generally have less of an impact on your blood glucose levels. As a general rule, people who eat a lot of low-glycemic-index foods tend to have lower levels of total body fat. Foods with a low glycemic index include most vegetables, whole grains, legumes, and some fruits.

As I touched on in my previous discussion of breads, there are good and not-so-good carbohydrates, which affect our blood sugar levels in different ways. Numerous studies on the effect of glucose levels, weight loss, and diabetes have explored the body's response to carbohydrates. Foods with a high glycemic index can result in weight gain and poor blood sugar levels. For a more healthful diet and greater weight loss, focus on eating more foods with a low glycemic index.

You might want to carry with you a list of high- and low-glycemic-index foods. You can refer to it when you go grocery shopping or eat out. Eventually, you'll get the hang of what is considered high and low, and that knowledge will help you control your weight.

In the following lists, various foods' glycemic indexes are based on glucose, which is one of the fastest (quickly converted into blood sugar) carbohydrates available. Glucose is given a value of 100, and other carbs are given a number relative to glucose. Note that these numbers are compiled from a wide range of research sources. You should use these numbers only as a general guideline. The impact a food will have on the blood sugar also depends on many other factors, such as the following:

- Cooking time
- Fiber amount
- Fat content
- Time of day the food is eaten
- Other foods eaten at the same time
- Amount of protein in the food
- The way the food was prepared
- Your own body's reaction to the food, such as your blood insulin levels while eating and your recent activity (for example, you just woke up or just completed working out)

All of these factors affect how your body responds to different glycemic levels in foods. Use the index as just one of the many tools you have available to improve your control of your weight. You can find lists of low- (good), medium-, and high- (bad) glycemic index foods in many books. Choose foods with a low or medium glycemic index as often as you can. Avoid foods with a high glycemic index.

If you do not want to carry a list with you when you shop or go out to eat, keep this general guideline in mind:

- Unprocessed foods tend to have lower glycemic indexes than refined or packaged foods.
- Some packaged food products will list their relative glycemic number, although it is not required.

Glycemic Indexes

Low (good) glycemic index: 55 or less
Medium glycemic index: 56–69
High (bad) glycemic index: 70 or higher

Glycemic Indexes of Common Foods

Raisin bran 73	Frosted flakes 55
Cheerios 74	Oatmeal, old-fashioned 48
Corn flakes 83	Cream of Wheat 66
Bagel 72	Doughnut 76
Oatmeal cookie 57	Corn chips 72
Potato chips 56	French fries 75
Baked potato 85	Sweet potato 54
Pretzels 83	Saltine crackers 74
Gatorade 78	Water 0
Baked beans 48	Apples 38
Table sugar 64	Honey 62

Tips for Using the Glycemic Index

As you can see, some foods that you may have thought are healthful may in fact be causing you to hold some extra weight. Making more healthful choices doesn't mean sacrificing taste. It's easy enough to eat a sweet potato rather than a baked potato or to choose long-grain over short-grain rice or brown rice over white rice as a general rule. And make sure you eat some protein with these carbohydrate-rich foods to help balance out your blood sugar level.

Take the following steps when you are eating to ensure a more stable blood sugar level:

- Include one medium- or low-glycemic food per meal.
- Eat higher-fiber foods with your meals to help break down higher-glycemic foods.
- Add protein and fat to your meal. This will help lower the glycemic levels of your meal.
- Do not eat a high- or medium-glycemic food right before bedtime. This step will prevent spikes in your blood sugar.

CHAPTER SUMMARY

- Clean up your eating habits. The effort will pay you dividends of more energy and a healthier lifestyle.
- Try a variety of foods at every meal.
- Make an effort to use vegetables as your focal point in at least one meal per day or week.
- Replace red meat and chicken with fish once or twice per week.
- Add more fiber to your diet beyond the bowl of cereal in the morning.
- Watch the glycemic index of the foods that you eat. Combine foods to have better control of your blood sugar levels and improve the way you feel and look.

CHAPTER 10

BEAT THE BLOAT FOR A FLATTER STOMACH

Your body is exposed to foreign chemicals on a daily basis, and many of these can result in uncomfortable and unsightly bloating. Studies have shown that the more toxins to which the body is exposed, the more difficulty it has detoxifying itself. Reducing exposure to toxins helps not only by decreasing toxicity directly, but also by increasing your body's ability to defend itself against existing toxins.

To help you decrease bloating for an even slimmer waistline, we will first look at probiotics that aid in restoring and maintaining a healthy intestinal balance in favor of healthful bacteria, which are essential for maintaining good health. Later in this chapter, we will look at food allergens and their role in disrupting the delicate balance going on in your digestive tract to help explain why some people have frequent bloating episodes and how to keep that from happening.

BEWARE OF BACTERIA

More than a trillion bacteria inhabit your body. And they aren't just silent partners. They digest your food, make vitamins, protect you from pathogens, and can even affect your weight and appetite. There are over two pounds of bacteria living inside your colon. These organisms metabolize bile acids, break down indigestible parts of your food, and produce vitamins. A recent study identified a strain capable of contributing to obesity by disrupting the appetite-regulating hormone ghrelin. And you were just scared that bacteria make our hands dirty!

Your gastrointestinal tract has trillions of microbes, and they are all involved with your current stomach condition, including the inflammatory response—think bloating or ballooning past your belt line after a meal or even when waking up in the morning before you have eaten. There is a growing recognition of the numerous benefits of taking dietary supplements like probiotics (which promote healthy bacteria) as a means of inflammation control and intestinal re-inoculation.

HOW WE INGEST BACTERIA

Our modern-day lifestyle provides us with an endless array of instant food choices from restaurants and vending machines. Of course, no one reading this book would ever grab something to eat out of a machine, but you can let your less-enlightened friends know what you learn in this chapter and steer them toward a healthier lifestyle.

The Usual Suspects

Here are a few of the most common items that disrupt the balance in our intestinal tract and bring unfriendly bacteria into our bodies:

- Processed foods
- Foods sprayed with chemicals
- Foods infused with antibiotics
- Improperly handled food sources
- Drugs, alcohol, tobacco, and caffeine

HOW BACTERIA WORK

Studies have provided us with a better understanding of how these bacteria function and their effects on your immune system, as well as how our gastrointestinal, or GI, response (swelling) affects our health, not to mention our midsection's girth. Even if it seems like a stretch to completely absorb the topic of digestive health while you're thinking about new ways of working your abs, don't skip this chapter. If you want to build a stronger and leaner body, you have to learn about the trillions of microbes in your digestive tract.

Without getting bogged down too much in the science and the relationship of bacteria in your gut lining, we will focus on a few major microbes and their effect on your intestines, along with ways to use this information to improve the way you feel and look. Keep in mind that microbes are not a single identity; rather, there are many different kinds, designed to do many different things in your GI tract to help restore balance and maintain consistent regularity, which helps reduce bloating and improves digestion.

GOOD VERSUS BAD BACTERIA: RESTORE THE BALANCE AND SHRINK YOUR WAIST

Recent research suggests that certain GI bacteria may be a cause of weight gain or the reason why people have difficulty dropping those last few pounds. Certain bacteria are better at breaking down certain nutrients, while others are really great at storing fat. Bacteria in the second category cause some people to absorb more calories from certain types of food than others, as well as store more of those calories as fat, thanks to the microbes in your intestinal lining.

A recent study by Washington University School of Medicine in St. Louis found a link between obesity and bacteria living in the intestine. The researchers focused on two major groups of bacteria—the Bacteroidetes and the Firmicutes—which together make up more than 90 percent of microbes found in the intestines of mice and humans. In the journal *Nature*, scientists have reported that obese mice had more Firmicutes in their intestinal tract than lean mice did, while lean mice had more Bacteroidetes in their intestinal tract than obese mice. In an earlier study, they compared genetically obese mice and lean mice. The obese mice had 50 percent fewer Bacteroidetes and a proportionate enhancement of Firmicutes.

Because people also differ in the amount of various kinds of intestinal bacteria, not every bowl of cereal may yield the same number of calories for two different people eating the same food. A person could pull out more or less energy from a food serving, depending upon their collection of intestinal microbes.

This is especially so for digesting carbohydrates. These trillions of friendly microbes help digest food the body can't on its own, such as the complex sugars found in grains, fruits, and vegetables. As part of the digestive process, the microbes break down nutrients to extract calories that would otherwise be stored as fat.

In another article in *Nature*, Ruth E. Ley, Ph.D., reported that her investigation found a similar correlation for obese humans as well. As the patients lost weight, the abundance of Bacteroidetes increased, and the abundance of Firmicutes decreased, irrespective of the diet subjects were on.

Knowing what we know about certain bacteria raises an important question: Are some of us born predisposed to become obese or overweight? Or does our diet over the years possibly influence the changes that occur in our intestinal flora?

While more studies need to be conducted, there is evidence that maintaining good bacteria in your gastrointestinal tract may help you get lean through better absorption of nutrients to help prevent fat storage and strengthen your body. You can do this by taking probiotics and probiotic supplements.

NORMALIZING YOUR GASTROINTESTINAL FUNCTION

Deficiencies of digestive enzymes and the imbalances in the gastrointestinal pH are all-too-common causes of impaired digestion, contributing to malabsorption of nutrients, food intolerance, and food allergy and toxicity. Foods that are not completely digested can putrify or ferment in your intestine, resulting in the production of endotoxins that cause excessive bloating and discomfort. Normalizing your intestinal function by using probiotics daily will improve your digestion, reduce toxins, and improve your overall environment.

PROBIOTICS: INCREASE GOOD BACTERIA

Probiotics are friendly bacteria that are predominately found in the upper intestinal tract. They help reduce the levels of harmful bacteria and yeast in the small intestine and also produce lactase, an enzyme important in breaking down dairy foods.

Positive Effects of Probiotics
- Reduced inflammatory responses
- Reduced allergic reactions (for example, to food pesticides, additives, food coloring)
- Decreased toxic buildup from pathogenic bacteria
- Prevention of intestinal infections
- Detoxification of the large intestine and promotion of regular bowel movements
- Better digestion of lactose (milk sugar)

Probiotic Supplements

Supplementing your diet with *Lactobacillus acidophilus* and *Bifidobacterium bifidus* will help prevent bloating and gas buildup in your upper and lower intestinal tract. While there are many more subgroups and types of probiotics in our intestinal tract, these two probiotics have been studied the most, and the use of supplements concentrate on them for the best reduction of intestinal distress.

Lactobacillus acidophilus. *Lactobacillus*, better known simply as acidophilus, is a species of friendly bacteria predominately found in the upper intestinal tract. They help reduce the levels of harmful bacteria and yeast in the small intestine and also produce lactase, an enzyme important for breaking down dairy foods, such as cheese, milk, creams, and sauces with dairy components. Important by-products of acidophilus are B vitamins, including folic acid and niacin, produced when your food is being broken down in your digestive tract.

Bifidobacterium bifidus. *Bifidobacterium bifidus* is another species of friendly bacteria that predominately reside in the lower intestine. Like acidophilus, this type of bacteria helps break down lactose and other milk sugars. *Bifidobacterium bifidus* helps keep the pH in your intestinal tract at a level necessary to prevent candida (a yeast) and other parasites from taking over your system.

Probiotics in Yogurt

Yogurt, like wine and cheese, is put through a process that allows thousands of bacteria to do their jobs to create the finished product, be it a great-tasting glass of wine or a well-aged cheese. When yogurt is pasteurized, the process kills off any pathogenic bacteria that may be in the culture. In making yogurt, the species *Streptococcus thermophilus* and *Lactobacillus bulgaricus* are added to the product with the flavoring agents after pasteurization.

How do you know if any good bacteria are left behind? You can read the label to make sure your yogurt has probiotics to help beat the bloat. The words "Live and Active Cultures" tell you that the product contains at least 10 million bacteria per gram, or 2 billion in an 8-ounce cup. (A label that says, "Made with active cultures" is not the same; all milk starts that way before it is made into yogurt.)

So if you enjoy eating your yogurt, it makes sense to take a closer look at what you are actually eating and why you are eating it.

Choosing the Right Probiotics

The key to the success of probiotic nutrition is to understand that probiotic strains vary greatly and their impact hinges upon the specificity of the strains used and the method of culturing, purity, viability, packaging, and handling of the product to beneficially affect your intestinal microbial balance.

Here are a few pointers to keep in mind when purchasing probiotics. Although researching the following points is time consuming, making a one-time effort could go a long way in ensuring you obtain an effective, high-quality product. The best probiotic supplements come in powdered or capsule form and should be kept refrigerated. Look for supplements that contain lactobacillus, acidophilus, and bifidobacteria in the billions. Probiotics lose potency with age, so buy smaller quantities more often to ensure you are getting the most active cultures. If your probiotic supplements are effective, you should begin to feel a difference within a week or two. If not, try a different variety, combination, or brand the next month. Like everything else, even the best probiotics are no substitute for good overall healthful eating. But they do work extremely well as part of a balanced approach, combined with a healthful diet and exercise program.

Look at the following qualities when investigating a supplement for probiotics:

- **Shelf life.** Storage of the product is important in maintaining viability. Temperature, moisture, light, and air can all damage your probiotics. These variables can be controlled through the use of amber glass containers to prevent entry of oxygen, moisture, and light. Most importantly, refrigeration of the product is critical in ensuring the potency of the bacterial strains.
- **Safety.** The product should come from a reliable manufacturer.
- **Colony count.** It should be very high for money wisely spent and usually is listed on the label; if not, pass it up. Look for colony counts in the billions as a good starting point for purchasing.
- **Intestinal adhesion properties.** Are you able to stomach the product? Give your body at least one week to adjust to the new probiotic before changing products.

When to Take Probiotics

The best time to take probiotics is first thing in the morning, before your breakfast. If you are unable to do it then, the next best time is half an hour before your last meal of the day.

FACTORS THAT AFFECT THE BALANCE OF FRIENDLY BACTERIA AND LEAD TO BLOATING

Our lifestyle plays a vital role in the homeostasis of our digestive tract as well as our overall health. The following factors commonly throw our system out of balance.

- **Antibiotic effects.** If you are or have been a heavy user of antibiotics over the years, you may have noticed an increase in bloating after you use the antibiotics. Not only do these drugs kill off the bad bacteria, they kill good bacteria as well, thus causing a deficiency in your intestinal tract. True, your body will produce more healthy bacteria on its own; we have survived without supplements for many centuries. With that said, why wait around for your body to produce the good bacteria when you can easily help your body's immune response by adding the good microflora to your system, thus reducing the swelling and discomfort involved? However, do not use any probiotic product, be it yogurt or a supplement, while taking an antibiotic; you'll decrease the potency of the antibiotic.

- **Poor diet.** A diet high in fat and low in fiber makes it difficult for your body to regulate and maintain your healthy bacteria in this type of environment.
- **Travel abroad.** Traveling outside of your own country increases your risk of being exposed to different bacteria and possible parasites.
- **Contamination.** From our food and water sources, we can unknowingly pick up foreign by-products that affect our gastrointestinal system.

Now that you know how to avoid the bloat caused by bacteria, let's look at some of the other hidden dangers lurking unseen in the foods that you eat.

IS SODIUM CAUSING YOUR BLOATING AND SWELLING?

Do you appear fatter on some days than others, even if you have eaten the same amount and type of foods as the day before? Perhaps the culprit is sodium. Too much sodium forces your cells to pull in fluid from the outside, which causes swelling, which is different from true fat made up of adipose tissue. Because your body is made up of 65 to 70 percent water, even slight changes in the volume of your water can make a huge difference in your weight and appearance.

Your muscles themselves are made up of 75 percent water. Your body is constantly trying to maintain equilibrium throughout your entire system by flushing water through your liver and gastrointestinal tract to process and to help eliminate foods, while water is used to filter out toxins and other minerals through your kidneys.

Too much sodium can leave you dehydrated. When that happens, you are forcing your body's organs to work harder to maintain this sensitive balance. Thus, it's important to remain hydrated, so your body can flush your system and work at its optimum ability. Keep in mind that you also lose

water through sweating—more so when you are working out. This delicate
balance is affected by the food we eat as well.

193 ■
Beat the Bloat for
a Flatter Stomach

FOOD SENSITIVITY AND FOOD REACTIONS

Eating the wrong food can cause you to retain fluid by triggering an inflammatory response from your body, which results in fluid retention and swelling as the food passes through your system, particularly your intestinal tract, and your tissues respond by bloating. These food triggers cause your adrenal glands to react to the inflammation by releasing hormones like adrenaline and cortisol, which put additional stress on your body, making your organs retain sodium and other minerals that swell within the tissues.

Women are familiar with premenstrual swelling and false weight gain. But men and women equally produce intestinal hormones that bring about swelling and cause sodium and minerals such as calcium to be absorbed by your tissues.

Your food reactions can cause severe gas production by producing abnormal bacteria and yeast, which leads to fermentation of the food in the gut lining. Fermentation is primarily a process following ingestion of carbohydrates, and it forms bloating and gas. These adverse responses to the toxic food cause the whole digestive process to slow down, squeezing rather than flowing through your digestive tract, slowing the complete bowel function. This results in further gas production and swelling. The entire progression causes a swollen and distended belly, not true fat.

What Causes This Food Reaction?

The number one cause of most food reactions is having indigestible foods trapped in your body. At almost every meal, most people eat certain foods that do not get completely digested. The results are beyond a bellyache. Foods you cannot digest will almost always trigger some reaction from your body.

The food that is not processed properly can enter your digestive tract in a large mass, which wreaks havoc on your system. Your body perceives these undigested masses as foreign invaders, similar to bacteria, viruses, and even parasites. The result is that your immune system kicks in and responds with an inflammatory response to this foreign body failing to break down in your digestive tract. The following symptoms are noticeable when your body responds this way:

- Bloating
- Swelling
- Heartburn (indigestion)
- False sense of fullness
- Fatigue

Causes of Incomplete Digestion

Incomplete digestion is most likely to occur when we eat processed foods, a limited variety of foods, and foods that are not in season.

Processed Foods. Too many of us eat foods that are not in their natural form. In this synthetic processing, the artificial sweeteners and fake fats added to our foods act as foreign substances in our digestive tract. Look closely at anything you buy at the grocery store that comes in a package. There are usually many additives and preservatives to keep these products looking and tasting the way they do for a very long time. Is it any wonder why we can't digest these foods completely? Preservatives, by their very nature, are designed to kill things. Specifically, they work by killing cells and preventing them from multiplying and are intended to prevent the growth of bacteria and fungi in commercial food products.

For example, sulfur is used to keep dried fruit fresh. Formaldehyde is added to disinfect frozen vegetables. Sodium nitrate is commonly used in the preservation of ham, bacon, sausage, and bologna to keep meat looking red, when normally it would have decomposed into an unappealing gray. In the stomach, sodium nitrate is converted into nitrous acid, which is suspected of inciting stomach cancer. Norway and other European countries have banned the use of this powerful toxin.

Limited Food Choices. Stop reading for a moment, and write down what you have eaten today. Now write down what you ate yesterday and, if you can think back, what you ate two days ago. I'm willing to bet that some of the same foods keep popping up, day after day. There are so many different types of foods available to us; why do we limit our diets so narrowly? Some of your habitual foods may be causing you to bloat and react adversely, as overeating any particular food can exhaust your body's ability to fully digest the food source.

Eating Foods Out of Season. Have you noticed that you can buy just about any type of produce year round? There are no longer cycles or seasons for the fruits and vegetables we consume these days. We get our foods from farther and farther locations where the temperature is ideal for growing while we have stopped producing them in our country due to the colder seasons. For preservation, these foods are picked and shipped quickly, before they fully ripen, or they are full of pesticides that cause adverse body responses. A solution is to eat locally and, if you can, choose organic foods that will help manage your body's stomach response.

FOOD ADDITIVES AND PRESERVATIVES

Food additives have been used for centuries. Salt, sugar, and vinegar were among the first ingredients used to preserve foods. During the past 30 years, however, with the arrival of processed foods, there has been an enormous amount of chemical adulteration of foods with additives. Considerable controversy has been associated with the potential threats and possible benefits of food additives.

Additives

Any substance that becomes part of a food product through processing, storage, or packaging is considered an additive. Food additives include colorings, flavors, sweeteners, texture agents, and other processing agents. Some additives are manufactured from natural sources, such as soybeans and corn, which provide lecithin to maintain product consistency, or beets, which provide beet powder used as food coloring. Other additives are manufactured. Artificial additives can be produced more economically, with greater purity and more consistent quality, than some of their natural counterparts.

Regardless of how they are added to the food product, your body has a similar reaction to food additives. You store these additives in your intestinal lining, disrupting the absorption of nutrients and vitamins while at the same time creating an inhospitable environment for your normal flora. The results include bloating.

Preservatives

A preservative is any additive that extends a food's freshness or shelf life. Preservatives are substances added to foods by manufacturers to prevent spoilage or to improve appearance, taste, texture, or nutritive value. They have been known to cause food sensitivities in people.

A common preservative to watch out for is hydrogenated oils (also known as trans fats or trans-fatty acids). This preservative increases the shelf life and flavor stability of foods containing polyunsaturated fats. Hydrogenated fats, also know as trans fats, are associated with many serious diseases such as cancer, atherosclerosis, diabetes, obesity, and immune system dysfunction. They have also been found to contribute to cardiovascular disease, such as fat-clogged arteries.

There are other fats to be aware of because they affect your health, and some help keep inflammation from occurring:

- Saturated fats are hard at room temperature. These fats are not essential to your health. They come from animals and are found in meat, eggs, and cheese.
- Unsaturated fats—"the good guys"—are generally anti-inflammatory and are liquid at room temperature. They have been divided into two groups: monounsaturated fats, such as olive oil, and polyunsaturated fats such as sunflower oil.

SMART SHOPPING TO AVOID CHEMICAL REACTIONS

There are a number of steps you can take to avoid causing chemical reactions in your body, thus preventing the unpleasant side effects of bloating, gas, and weight gain. The most important step is to buy foods as close as possible to their natural form. Sure, we would like to eat strawberries all year round, but not at the price of increasing our waistlines and ingesting all those chemicals. Be sure to buy fruits and vegetables in season. If you cannot do that, then buy your produce frozen without added coloring or preservatives.

Another important tip is to buy organic as much as possible within your budget. A report by the nonprofit Environmental Working Group has identified the conventionally grown vegetables and fruits that are the most contaminated and least contaminated with pesticides. You can avoid many of these chemicals and their adverse reactions by eating fewer of the ones in the following list of most-contaminated produce and eating more from the list of the less-contaminated vegetables and fruits.

Most Contaminated
- Apples
- Bell peppers
- Celery
- Cherries
- Imported grapes
- Nectarines
- Peaches
- Pears
- Potatoes
- Spinach
- Strawberries

Least Contaminated
- Asparagus
- Avocados
- Bananas
- Broccoli
- Cauliflower
- Onions
- Pineapples
- Sweet corn
- Sweet peas

The safest thing to do is to avoid all foods that contain any additives whatsoever. The easiest way to do this is to eat only those foods that have been organically produced and are certified as such by a reputable organic certification body. This need not be any more expensive than buying other kinds of food, though, regrettably, many organic growers and suppliers tend to take advantage of the situation and charge high premiums for the privilege of eating safe food. You may have to search around and "negotiate," but it is the very best and safest route if you are able to take it.

If the organic option is not available to you, then you should learn as much as you can about the additives used in the foods you buy, and stay away from the ones that are the most threatening. A simple general rule about additives is to avoid sodium nitrite, saccharin, caffeine, olestra, and artificial colorings. Not only are they among the most questionable additives, but also they are used primarily in foods of low nutritional value. Also, don't forget the two most familiar additives: sugar and salt. They may pose the greatest threat because we consume so much of them, and the way our body reacts to these stimuli varies from day to day, meal to meal, causing gastrointestinal upset in many.

MILK AND LACTOSE INTOLERANCE

The ever-present milk mustache ads have claims of preventing osteoporosis and other problems. But if you are lactose intolerant, milk may be contributing to that bloat around your middle. Here are a few interesting facts:

- Among people of Hispanic descent, 50 to 60 percent are lactose intolerant.
- Among people of African descent, 65 to 70 percent are lactose intolerant.
- Among people of Italian descent, 65 to 70 percent are lactose intolerant.
- Among people of Native American descent, 95 percent are lactose intolerant.
- Among people of Caucasian descent, 10 percent are lactose intolerant.
- Among people of Asian descent, 90 to 100 percent are lactose intolerant.

The common symptoms of lactose intolerance are gastrointestinal, primarily abdominal pain, flatulence, diarrhea, abdominal bloating, abdominal distention, and nausea. Unfortunately, these symptoms can be caused by other gastrointestinal conditions or diseases, so the presence of these symptoms is not very good at predicting whether a person has lactase deficiency or lactose intolerance. Symptoms occur because unabsorbed lactose passes through the small intestine and into the colon, and not all of the lactose that reaches the colon is split and used by colonic bacteria. The result is bloating of the midsection.

The severity of the symptoms of lactose intolerance varies greatly from person to person. One reason for this variability is that people have different amounts of lactose in their diet; the more lactose in the diet, the more likely and severe the symptoms. Another reason for the variability is that people have differing severities of lactase deficiency, that is, they may have mildly, moderately, or severely reduced amounts of lactase in their intestines. Thus, small amounts of lactose will cause major symptoms in severely lactase-deficient people but only mild or no symptoms in mildly lactase-deficient people. Finally, people may have different responses to the same amount of lactose reaching the colon. Whereas some may have mild or no symptoms, others may have moderate symptoms. The reason for this is not clear but may relate to differences in their intestinal bacteria. In addition, antibiotics are allowed to be present in U.S. cow's milk.

So adding milk to your morning cereal or your coffee could be the culprit if you are feeling bloated. An alternative to cow's milk is soy milk. If you have never had it before, it can taste similar to skim milk.

Soy Milk

In China and Japan, fresh soy milk is made daily, using a simple, centuries-old process of grinding soaked and cooked soybeans and pressing the dissolved soy milk out of the beans. Soy milk is free of the milk sugar lactose and is a good choice for people who are lactose intolerant. Also, it is a good alternative for those who are allergic to cow's milk. It never contains antibiotics, as does cow's milk. Luckily, there are a number of brands on the market today to choose from.

Types of Soy Milk. Soy milk is available as a plain, unflavored beverage or in a variety of flavors, including chocolate and vanilla. With the growing interest in lower-fat products, a number of "light" soy milks, with reduced fat content, are appearing on the market.

Nutritional Value of Soy Milk. Plain, unfortified soy milk is an excellent source of high-quality protein, B vitamins, and iron. Some brands of soy milk are fortified with vitamins and minerals and are good sources of calcium, vitamin D, and vitamin B_{12}. One cup of soy milk contains about 25 milligrams of healthful isoflavones.

An additional bonus is the extra potassium you consume from including this food in your diet, improving the balance in your body's system.

CHAPTER SUMMARY

Improve your digestion with probiotics, which help reduce intestinal bloating and discomfort. They normalize your gastrointestinal function while delivering these benefits:

- Improving digestion
- Removing intestinal toxins
- Rebuilding intestinal mucosa
- Reestablishing normal intestinal flora
- Enhancing the immune system, improving resistance to infection, and improving well-being
- Possibly lowering serum cholesterol levels
- Reducing allergic inflammation

Reestablishing normal flora or bacteria by using beneficial bacteria supplements mentioned in this chapter contributes to a healthy intestinal environment by maintaining optimum pH levels and producing important nutrients. In addition, it suppresses the growth of pathogenic organisms and reduces their invasion of your gastrointestinal system, thus reducing the bloating and swelling of your midsection.

Besides using probiotics, you can help normalize your gastrointestinal function with the following practices:

- Read all the ingredients on the labels of foods you purchase, so you really know what you are putting into your body.
- Eliminate foods that are high in chemicals and fillers added for appearance rather than for nutritional value.
- Eat fruits and vegetables in season.
- Buy organic produce, dairy, and meats.

CHAPTER II

HOW YOU EAT IS JUST AS IMPORTANT AS WHAT YOU EAT

It's very easy to develop poor eating habits these days with our fast-paced lifestyles, leaving less time to relax and enjoy what we put into our mouths. There are so many ways to overeat without taking much thought about what you are doing if you are distracted by stimuli other than the food you are eating. So turn off your cell phone, close down your e-mails, and just read this chapter to help you reach a lifestyle that will make you healthier and feeling better.

OVEREATING AND OVERWEIGHT: WHICH CAME FIRST, THE CHICKEN OR THE EGG?

People overeat for many reasons. Is it possible to stop yourself from doing so, or is it a habit that's ingrained in your genetic makeup?

Why We Overeat

These factors are known to encourage overeating:

- A favorite food
- Alcohol

- Boredom
- Bringing your job stress home with you
- Eating your meals in your car
- Rushing to fit in a meal before running off to pick up the kids or get to work
- Hormones, including stress-triggered hormones that can increase appetite and cravings for unhealthful foods, as well as some women's experience of changes in eating habits in response to the hormonal flux of their menstrual cycles
- Social events, such as those where there is pressure to fit in by drinking too much
- The practice of not eating before going to events, so you have calories saved for the event, rather than eating normal-size meals
- Eating alone more often than with a group of friends or coworkers
- Eating to please someone else—having "one more piece"
- Belief that you're eating more healthfully than you are—for example, eating no-fat or low-fat foods throughout the day and then overeating at night because the supposedly healthful food choices didn't "count"

Instant Gratification

The most important and prevalent reason people tend to overeat is for pleasure. Eating makes us feel good, and when we do so on impulse, it is instantly gratifying. We do it because we see and smell food, or it is simply advertised, so we have to taste it. Millions of people are susceptible to the constant barrage of food invitations, which is why the Food Network is on 24 hours a day, daring all of us to attempt the preparation of mouthwatering, mega-calorie meals. Of course this affects the way you eat. Why do you think grocery stores put out samples of foods while you are shopping? Because it triggers the "why not?" syndrome. You don't even have to be hungry to enjoy it; you just have to be in proximity to the food in question.

BUY GROCERIES WITH TASTE AND HEALTH IN MIND

When I was growing up, I would go to the grocery store with my mother on most occasions when she'd buy the week's staples—the foods we had in our house all the time. But it was a real special treat to go with my father on a Saturday morning. We didn't really need anything, but he had a taste for something, he would say. It was on my father's special tour of tasting and shopping that I learned a number of things about consuming and enjoying foods.

First, we started on the right side of the store, where the deli was, and they would have samples of meats and cheeses with toothpicks ready to go, ours for the taking. Next we moved to the center of the store, where electric pans were heating samples of something that looked like rolled-up dough with liquid oozing out its side. It didn't matter if we were hungry or not; it was there to try.

After eating meat and cheese and baked goods, my father craved something salty. We would head down the snack aisle, where he would proceed to pick up several bags of chips and pretzels. Finally, we moved on to the produce section to sample the in-season fruits cut up, ours to take. We had just satisfied our major desires for tastes of protein, fat, salt, and sweets, all within one hour, and then my father would purchase some diet soda. Off we went without a care for calories, fat content, or carbohydrates.

The reason I share this with you is to help you focus on why and how you shop at the supermarket. Two different experiences I had with my parents shaped the way I purchased and consumed food later in life. Do you roam through the store, looking for new and exciting foods to eat? Or do you drone through the aisles, picking the same foods over and over again, year after year? To tone and shape your midsection, you need to eat a variety of food in small portions while satisfying your sense of taste, so you can stick with healthful eating habits.

SMART EATING HABITS

You can improve your eating habits by paying attention to what you're eating now. Use that information to target the improvements you want to make to your diet, such as stocking your pantry with easy and healthful choices. Following are more steps to ensure you make healthy food choices.

Keep a Food Log

If you aren't aware of everything that you put in your mouth, how are you ever going to drop the weight and shrink your waist? Start with a simple piece of paper, and place it on your bedroom nightstand. Why there? At first, I don't want you to think about what you are going to eat and should be eating. Instead, wait until the end of each day, and write down what you ate that day. Do that for 10 days straight. This will give you a truer reading of what you put in your mouth. It's basically the same as if someone is looking over your shoulder while you are doing something. This helps you in case you feel pressure to make changes before learning what you actually do eat.

Once you've kept your food diary for 10 days, go through it and label the different kinds of foods to get a sense of how much protein, fat, carbs, vegetables, fruit, bread, meat, fish, and drinks you consume each day. Look for patterns that emerge in the food diary. What kinds of food do you eat the most? What type of meat are you eating—burgers, steak? Do you always eat out on certain days of the week, and if so, are you eating the same foods on those days? Are you eating healthfully only at the beginning of the day and then cave in to what's the most convenient food later, without regard to nutritional value?

Once you have a sense of how you eat on a regular basis, you can build upon this information by consciously balancing out your proteins, fats, and carbs for a slimmer waistline and healthier eating habits.

Turn Up the Volume

Choose high-volume foods. The volume of a food refers to how much space a typical serving takes up. A low-volume food would be something like cheese, pizza, or a burger, which packs a lot of calories but not a whole lot of volume into your stomach. A salad with a lot of roughage and fiber would be considered a high-volume food, allowing you to feel fuller during the course of your meal. Slow down while you eat, and think of what you are putting into your mouth. Enjoy it!

Ditch the Junk Food

Studies of people's eating habits reveal that almost a quarter of the calories we consume come from nutrient-poor selections, better known as "junk food." If a quarter of what we eat is junk food, a plan for weight reduction should emphasize eating differently, not just eating less, as many nutrition experts advise for weight loss. And if you have a healthy weight, you should still eat less junk food, so you can stay that way.

Go Easy on the Sodas and Sweets

A study showed that people consumed more than 23 percent of their total calories for the day in the form of sodas and sweets. Not only is this a missed opportunity to eat or drink something more nutritious, but people who eat this way are causing their body to combat the effects of sugar—inflammation and bloating—and playing havoc with their metabolism by overloading it with chemicals, simple sugars, and corn syrup.

One of the dangers of junk food is that it displaces healthful food, even if you maintain an appropriate weight. Eating substantial amounts of high-calorie, low-nutrient foods tends to be part of an eating pattern that ignores nutrient-rich vegetables, fruits, whole grains, and beans. Even if eating lots of junk food doesn't cause you to gain weight, you could increase your health risks and susceptibility to disease by depriving your-self of protective nutrients. And of course, there are always better foods to snack on.

Healthy Snacking Is the Key to Your Success

While some dieters happily accept when offered a snack, others feel pangs of remorse when they even consider a bite to eat. However, there is nothing inherently wrong with a snack between meals. In fact, snacking might be the missing ingredient that will help you reach your weight loss goals. As long as you are not overloading on empty calories in the process, snacks can be quite beneficial. Remember, snacking doesn't serve to replace a meal; rather, it's a stopgap to keep you sated until the next one. Munching between meals can actually reduce your overall caloric intake by curbing overeating at your next meal. So the question, then, isn't whether or not to snack, but what foods you should snack on.

Lean toward foods that will satisfy your desire and keep you feeling fuller longer. Here are some ideas that do so nutritiously:

- Carrots, apples, or oranges are always a safe choice, because they are low in fat and calories.
- Nuts (cashews, walnuts, and almonds) are good snack foods. Just make sure you don't go overboard by eating more than an ounce or two, because a small amount packs a lot of calories.
- Low-fat, low-sodium turkey or chicken breast delivers protein, which will help you feel fuller longer.
- Edamame, with 7 grams of fiber, is a good source of fiber and protein.
- Low-fat string cheese or cottage cheese
- Hard-boiled eggs
- Celery sticks with peanut butter
- Broccoli
- Sandwiches made of turkey on whole wheat bread
- High-fiber cereal
- Mixed berries, such as blueberries and raspberries, or grapes
- Whole wheat crackers

The trick here is to be prepared and be creative with your choices every day. Buy your fresh fruits and vegetables on the weekend in preparation for the week's snacking. Keep small containers for packing small portions. Take note of the healthful foods you need to keep stocked in the house for future quick and healthful snack preparation. You will begin to notice that you start to replace a few calorie-wasting items with your new healthful snack.

Now that you are committed to eating healthful snacks and eating more planned meals, rather than eating on a whim, let's check out what you have on your kitchen shelves to help you lose weight and eat healthful foods. If you do not want to throw out food, give it away.

Items to Get Rid Of
- Salad dressings loaded with sugar or high in fat or sodium
- Artificial sweeteners
- White rice and pasta
- Chip dips
- White potatoes

Replacements
- Olive oil
- Nuts
- Sweet potatoes
- Whole wheat breads and grains
- Whole wheat pasta
- Brown rice
- Tomatoes when in season
- Oatmeal and other high-fiber cereals low in sugar and sodium
- Carrots
- Different types of lettuce
- Apples and oranges

These are just a few suggestions, and I know how hard it is to remove foods from your shelves, especially if you are like me and have kids around your house. If you can't win the battle of removing them from your home because of others, instead place a note in the location with a list of healthful alternative choices to help keep you from eating the junk food. Also, place a bowl of fruit out on the table or counter, so you can see a healthful choice before succumbing to an unhealthful snack.

Rethink the way you eat. Instead of three main meals, think of four or five smaller meals, spreading out your protein, carbohydrates, and fats through the entire day. If you eat at regular intervals, your blood sugar levels (and therefore your energy levels) remain stable without stressing your GI tract. Instead of that midafternoon crash, you'll feel more even-keeled and less irritable.

Remember, snacking is not grazing mindlessly, eating everything in sight just because the food is in small bites. The calories will add up and pack onto your waistline in no time. Do not eat directly out of any containers or boxed food products, continually reaching in to take handfuls without taking stock of what you have eaten already. Rather, remove the amount the box says is one serving, and place it on a plate or bowl. Limit yourself to a single serving, and remove the box from your sight to avoid temptation. Plan your snacks just as you would plan a meal. Is a handful of cookies worth the calories and saturated fat when you could eat a plate of vegetables or fresh fruit instead?

Practice Moderation

As with the rest of your diet, moderation is crucial when snacking. Make sure that you record every snack in your journal, along with the main meals you are eating during the day. If you don't keep track, you might add excess calories and fat to your diet without realizing it.

Don't sabotage your goals with unhealthful choices during the day and night. Stick to nourishing foods most of the time, and give into an occasionally unhealthful snack once a week if you must, and then really enjoy it. With less and less snacking on unhealthful foods, you will not crave them as much, and your body will not be in a state of flux, fighting inflammation caused by the nonnutritional components of unhealthful snacks. Eventually, the result of moderation will be a slimmer waistline.

Eating on the Go

In our society, eating no longer is an activity experienced only while sitting at the table. Quickly think about how many times this past week you have eaten while in a hurry. How many times have you eaten in your car, on the train ride into work, or at your desk? Your time is precious, and you need food that's easy to grab, easy to store, and easy to handle while being at least somewhat nutritious at the same time. Unfortunately, what falls into the "fast" and "easy" categories is mostly the bad stuff: chips, candy bars, sodas, and so on. The best way to fight on-the-go cravings is with healthful snacks like the ones listed earlier, prepared ahead of time and popped into a lunch bag. I'm talking about things that can fit into your top drawer at work (besides Ho Hos or chocolate kisses). Yes, these items may require some planning ahead. Some might even require refrigeration or special containers. But they are fast, simple, and easy. Most take less than five minutes to prepare.

You'll also be thankful that you've saved yourself some cash that normally goes to vending machines or convenience stores. Your body will be grateful as well. The benefits of health far outweigh the costs.

Curb Your Evening Eating

Do you eat mindlessly more at work or at home? Using your food log, follow a week's worth of eating. Look at what you have eaten, and mark which meal had protein, fats, carbohydrates, and the most calories. For many people, the hardest habits to change include eating a lot of food after dinner. The effect of eating late at night is that you are overloading your GI system with calories but not moving your body afterward, thus slowing your metabolism in the process.

Ask yourself the following questions:

- How many meals or snacks did you eat after 7:00 P.M.?
- How many meals and snacks did you eat during the day?
- How many total calories did you consume after 7:00 P.M.?
- How many total calories did you consume for the entire day?
- What physical activities did you engage in after eating at 7:00 P.M.?

If you consume more than one-third of your meals, snacks, and total calories after 7:00 P.M., then you need to take action to get your eating habits under control to help you achieve the waistline of your dreams and your desired weight.

Here's how you can do it. Try these steps to help fend off hunger:

- Maintain a regular time you go to sleep and wake up, even on the weekends.
- Establish a regular, relaxing bedtime routine.

- Finish eating at least two to three hours before going to sleep.
- Avoid caffeine and alcohol two hours before retiring for the night.

WEIGHT MANAGEMENT TIPS TO REACH YOUR GOALS

Now that you know how to eat healthfully the AbSmart way, it's time to map out some eating strategies to help you reach your goal of a firmer midsection and an ideal weight.

- In general, a healthy and reasonable calorie goal for weight loss is 10 times your goal weight (for example, 10×170 pounds = 1,700 calories per day). Add at least 10 percent to your daily calories if you exercise regularly. But adjust your food intake downward on the days that you cannot exercise; otherwise, you'll eat more calories than you burned that day.

- Set achievable and reasonable weight goals. A 10 to 15 percent weight loss in overweight individuals can produce dramatic health benefits, including reduction in blood pressure and blood cholesterol plus reduction in risk for diabetes and heart disease, but not in one month's time. Remember how long it took you to arrive at the weight you are now.

- Another good way to measure your progress, as well as determine which foods cause you to swell, is to measure your waistline in inches. Start by measuring the smallest part of your waist without sucking in your stomach. A waist measurement greater than 35 inches for females indicates you are overweight or have extreme bloating. A waist measurement of more than 40 inches for men places you in the danger zone for heart disease and diabetes.

- Your waist-to-hip ratio also helps to pinpoint how you store your excess weight. To determine your waist-to-hip ratio, measure around the smallest part of your waistline. Then measure your hips at the widest point. Divide your waist measurement by your hip measurement. If your waist-

Weight (Pounds)

Height	100	110	120	130	140	150	160	170	180	190	200	210	220	230	240	250
5'0"	20	21	23	25	27	29	31	33	35	37	39	41	43	45	47	49
5'1"	19	21	23	25	26	28	30	32	34	36	38	40	42	43	45	47
5'2"	18	20	22	24	26	27	29	31	33	35	37	38	40	42	44	46
5'3"	18	19	21	23	25	27	28	30	32	34	35	37	39	41	43	44
5'4"	17	19	21	22	24	26	27	29	31	33	34	36	38	39	41	43
5'5"	17	18	20	22	23	25	27	28	30	32	33	35	37	38	40	42
5'6"	16	18	19	21	23	24	26	27	29	31	32	34	36	37	39	40
5'7"	16	17	19	20	22	23	25	27	28	30	31	33	34	36	38	39
5'8"	15	17	18	20	21	23	24	26	27	29	30	32	33	35	36	38
5'9"	15	16	18	19	21	22	24	25	27	28	30	31	32	34	35	37
5'10"	14	16	17	19	20	22	23	24	26	27	29	30	32	33	34	36
5'11"	14	15	17	18	20	21	22	24	25	26	27	28	30	32	33	35
6'0"	14	15	16	18	19	20	22	23	24	26	27	28	30	31	33	34
6'1"	13	15	16	17	18	20	21	22	24	25	26	28	29	30	32	33
6'2"	13	14	15	17	18	19	21	22	23	24	26	27	28	30	31	32
6'3"	12	14	15	16	17	19	20	21	22	24	25	26	27	29	30	31
6'4"	12	13	15	16	17	18	19	21	22	23	24	26	27	28	29	30

Body Mass Index

to-hip ratio is 0.8 or greater, you are considered overweight; anything less than 0.8 is considered in the normal zone.

Figure Out Your BMI

Your body mass index (BMI) is a number derived from your weight and height. To determine your BMI, divide your weight in pounds by your height in inches, squared, and then multiply the resulting number by 703. For example, if you weigh 150 pounds and stand 5 feet 5 inches (65 inches) tall, you would calculate your BMI as follows:

$$150 \div (65 \times 65) = 0.0355$$
$$0.0355 \times 703 = 24.956$$

If you're simply not a math wizard and plugging in formulas brings back nightmares of your school days, you can get a rough idea of your BMI by using the chart. The pounds have been rounded off.

Once you know your BMI, you can use it to see if you're underweight, in the normal range, or overweight:

- A body mass index of less than 18.5 is considered underweight.
- A BMI between 18.5 and 24.9 is considered normal.
- A BMI of 25 or greater is considered overweight, and 30 or more is obese.

Heart disease, diabetes, and high blood pressure are all linked to being overweight.

Recommended Target Weight Loss

While you are slimming down to your ideal body weight, I recommend you aim to lose an average of a pound a week. Some weeks, you'll certainly lose more, especially at the beginning of your program, as you eliminate many foods that are causing your bloating and causing you to retain water. Other weeks, you will probably hit a plateau and will need to look at your food diary to see if you have added a certain type of food or left out any while you are making progress.

A pound of fat contains around 3,600 calories. To lose that pound in one week, you must reduce your caloric intake by around 550 calories per day (because 550 calories × 7 days = 3,850 calories cut in a week). At this rate, if you want to lose 20 pounds, it will take roughly 18 to 20 weeks (4 to 5 months).

Here's an example: A person who currently weighs 180 pounds wants to lose 18 pounds. To lose this weight at the rate of a pound a week, he or she must reduce calorie consumption by around 3,850 calories per week for 18 weeks.

This simple math can help you evaluate your food choices, so you can know how much you are really putting into your body. Also, this information should allow you to see how cutting calories will work for you. If you hit a plateau, you can see where you went off course.

CHAPTER SUMMARY

Invest in the time, energy, healthful ingredients, and good habits that will help you achieve your waist reduction goals:

- Invest in writing down everything you eat in your food log, so you can understand how your body reacts (bloating, cramps) to certain types of foods.
- Invest in not overeating at night.
- Invest in fresh produce and other fresh foods.
- Invest in reading cookbooks and trying recipes that feature fresh produce, lean meats, and whole grains.
- Invest in storage containers, a great source of convenience when you want to prepare fast, healthful food.
- Invest in a few minutes to toss out all those pizza coupons in your house.

CONCLUSION

Now that you are armed with the AbSmart system, I hope you will let it serve as a continual source of motivation and guidance, setting you on a course for a lifetime of a stronger midsection and extraordinary fitness. As you can see, AbSmart offers an enormous array of possibilities for your workouts, allowing you to strive toward advanced levels of physical training. But remember, the challenge begins with you. Using all the guidelines that this book has to offer you, move intelligently, using one movement to build upon the next before going on to more advanced exercises.

A lean midsection takes a combination of good nutrition, aerobic conditioning, and cardio and core training. We all wish we could spot-reduce by increasing our abdominal exercises, but it will not happen to you if you drink endless calories and eat yourself silly. If you clean up your diet and incorporate the food suggestions in this book, you'll be on your way to a leaner and firmer midsection.

If you train right, challenging yourself and eating well, you will be able to perform at your optimal level each time you exercise or compete in a sporting event.

Conversely, if you fail to challenge yourself or if you push too hard too quickly, you will undermine your efforts and become discouraged by doing the exercises halfheartedly and eating poorly as a result of frustration. Listen to your body: push when you feel strong, go easy when you cannot give 100 percent, and adapt to your emotional as well as your physical well-being. If you do that, you will achieve your goals.

With this book, my aim is to address the mechanisms of exercising your midsection and to show you how you can have challenging and fun workouts in a short period of time without doing endless repetitions of crunches. I hope you have learned a few new movements to add to your routine, and I wish you the best of health.

Keep on training!

REFERENCES

Arciero PJ, Gardner AW, Calles-Escandon J, Benowitz NL, Poehlman ET. Effects of caffeine ingestion on NE kinetics, fat oxidation, and energy expenditure in younger and older men. *Am. J. Physiol.* 1995; 268: E1192–98.

Begley, S. The end of antibiotics. *Newsweek*, March 28, 1994, pp. 47–51.

Bell DG, McLellan TM. Effect of repeated caffeine ingestion on repeated exhaustive exercise endurance. *Med. Sci. Sports Exerc.* 2003; 35:1348–54.

Conway KJ, Orr R, Stannard SR. Effect of a divided caffeine dose on endurance cycling performance, post exercise urinary caffeine concentration, and plasma paraxanthine. *J. Appl. Physiol.* 2003; 94:1557–62.

Costill DL, Dalsky GP, Fink WJ. Effects of caffeine ingestion on metabolism and exercise performance. *Med. Sci. Sports Exerc.* 1978; 10:155–58.

Flatz G. Genetics of lactose digestion in humans. In Harris H, Hirschhorn K, eds., *Advances in Human Genetics*. New York: Plenum, 1987.

Iacono G, et al. Intolerance of cow's milk and chronic constipation in children. *New Engl. J. Med.* 1998; 339:110–14.

Jacobs I, Pasternak H, Bell DG. Effects of ephedrine, caffeine, and their combination on muscular endurance. *Med. Sci. Sports Exerc.* 2003; 35:987–94.

Juneja LR, Chu D-C, Okubo T, et al. L-theanine: A unique amino acid of green tea and its relaxation effect in humans. *Trends Food Sci. Tech.* 1999; 10:199–204.

Kaduka T, Nozawa A, Unno T, et al. Inhibiting effects of theanine on caffeine stimulation evaluated by EEG in the rat. *Biosci. Biotechnol. Biochem.* 2000; 64:287–93.

Kitaoka S, Hayashi H, Yokogoshi H, Suzuki Y. Transmural potential changes associated with the in vitro absorption of theanine in the guinea pig intestine. *Biosci. Biotechnol. Biochem.* 1996; 60:1768–71.

Paluska SA. Caffeine and exercise. *Curr. Sports Med. Rep.* 2003; 2:213–19.

Sadzuka Y, Sugiyama T, Miyagishima A, et al. The effects of theanine, as a novel biochemical modulator, on the antitumor activity of adriamycin. *Cancer Lett.* 1996; 105:203–209.

Sadzuka Y, Sugiyama T, Sonobe T. Efficacies of tea components on doxorubicin induced antitumor activity and reversal of multidrug resistance. *Toxicol. Lett.* 2000; 113:155–62.

Scrimshaw NS, Murray EB. The acceptability of milk and milk products in populations with a high prevalence of lactose intolerance. *Am. J. Clin. Nutr.* 1988; 48:1083–85.

Spriet LL. Caffeine and performance. *Int. J. Sport Nutr.* 1995; 5 Suppl: S84–S99.

Spriet LL, MacLean DA, Dyck DJ, Hultman E, Cederblad G, Graham TE. Caffeine ingestion and muscle metabolism during prolonged exercise in humans. *Am. J. Physiol.* 1992; 262:E891–98.

Sugiyama T, Sadzuka Y. Enhancing effects of green tea components on the antitumor activity of adriamycin against M5076 ovarian carcinoma. *Cancer Lett.* 1998; 133:19–26.

Sugiyama T, Sadzuka Y. Combination of theanine with doxorubicin inhibits hepatic metastasis of M5076 ovarian sarcoma. *Clin. Cancer Res.* 1999; 5:413–16.

Sugiyama T, Sadzuka Y, Sonobe T. Theanine, a major amino acid in green tea, inhibits leukopenia and enhances antitumor activity induced by idarubicin. *Proc. Am. Assn. Cancer Res.* 1999; 40:10 (Abstract 63).

Yokogoshi H, Kobayashi M, Mochizuki M, Terashima T. Effect of theanine, r-glutamylethylamide on brain monoamines and striatal dopamine release in conscious rats. *Neurochem. Res.* 1998; 23:667–73.

INDEX

ABOUT THE AUTHOR

Adam Weiss is a board-certified chiropractic physician. Dr. Weiss graduated from National University of Health Sciences in 1992 and completed his clinical residency training at the Lombard and Chicago National Outpatient Centers. After completing undergraduate studies at Illinois State University, where he received a bachelor of science degree in biology and a bachelor of arts degree in chemistry, Dr. Weiss went on to graduate studies in mammal physiology at the University of Illinois. He was then accepted into the chiropractic program at National University of Health Sciences, a top-ranked chiropractic university in the United States. During his five-year program, he became a certified acupuncturist and received a bachelor of science degree in human biology and a doctor of chiropractic degree. In addition, Dr. Weiss has completed more than 1,800 hours of post-doctorate work in spinal rehabilitation, sports injuries, and nutrition.

Dr. Weiss has been in private practice for the past 16 years, specializing in neuromuscular injuries. As the medical director of Body by Pilates Fitness Center in Buffalo Grove, Illinois, Dr. Weiss has been successfully integrating the AbSmart and BackSmart methods, sports conditioning, and lifestyle changes including weight loss programs into his practice. Dr. Weiss's knowledge of endurance, flexibility, and strengthening exercises is a result of his own experience with martial arts and years of weight training. He has held a first-degree black belt in tae kwon do since the age of 15, having competed in state and national competitions at the junior and senior levels.

Dr. Weiss is highly sought after as a team physician for professional athletes and has worked with professional kickboxers, Olympic-level judo players, marathon runners, and golfers, all of whom depend on Dr. Weiss's unique programs and his advanced strengthening and conditioning exercises. Dr. Weiss works with these athletes and teaches Pilates reformer classes while maintaining a full-time practice. He also presents strengthening and conditioning exercises at workshops for professional and amateur sport clubs and martial arts studios throughout the United States.

Dr. Weiss's own experience with back pain at an early age forced him to modify and adapt exercise routines, resulting in more productive and effective forms of exercise for people of all ages. Dr. Weiss has also written *The Backsmart Fitness Plan: A Total-Body Workout to Strengthen and Heal Your Back*, a complete full-body workout. As a safe and progressive approach to the most effective exercises, the BackSmart method comprises hundreds of exercises, which allow a workout to be customized to meet individual needs. Dr. Weiss has also contributed to national magazines on health and fitness based on this system of toning and strengthening muscles—increasing aerobic endurance and improving posture, reducing joint and back stress, and reducing tension and stress in general. Dr. Weiss has also been interviewed on Project Health Radio on health and fitness based on this system.

When not seeing patients, teaching Pilates, writing, reading, and learning Japanese, he is experimenting with new exercises.

For information regarding seminars, classes, DVDs, and future books, please visit www.thebacksmart.com or search the Internet with the keywords *Dr. Adam Weiss, BackSmart*, or *AbSmart*.